The Official
Liverpool FC
Annual 2009

Written by Paul Eaton

A Grange Publication

© 2008. Published by Grange Communications Ltd., Edinburgh, under licence from Liverpool Football Club. Printed in the EU.

ISBN 978-1-906211-37-0

Photographs © David Rawcliffe/Propaganda.
LFC logo and crest are registered trademarks of The Liverpool Football Club and Athletic Grounds Ltd.

£6.99

Contents........

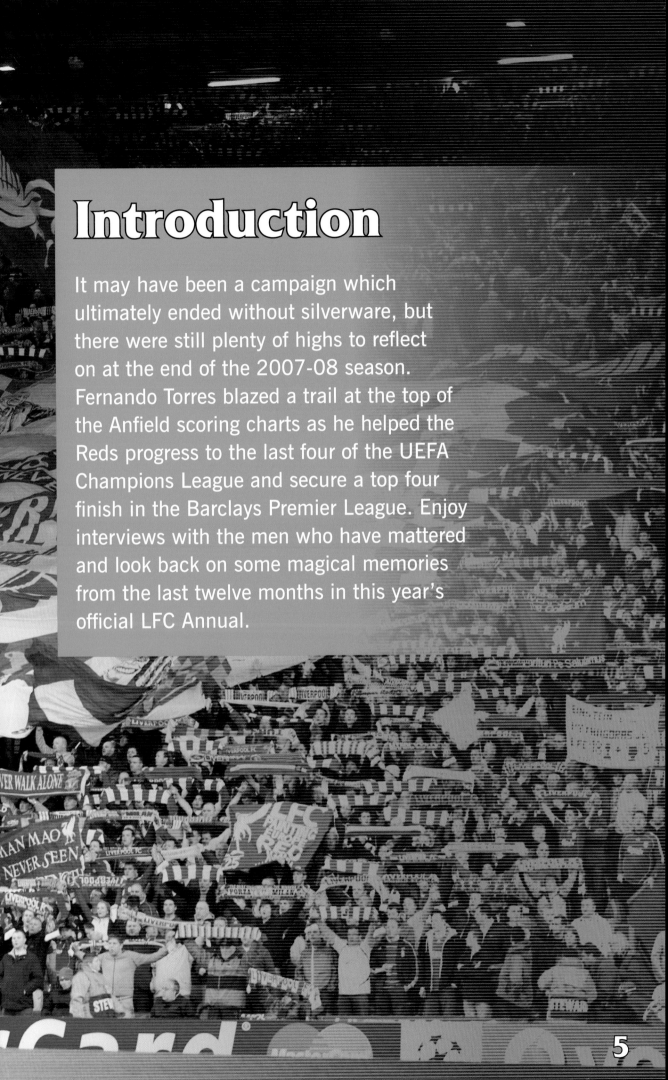

Introduction

It may have been a campaign which ultimately ended without silverware, but there were still plenty of highs to reflect on at the end of the 2007-08 season. Fernando Torres blazed a trail at the top of the Anfield scoring charts as he helped the Reds progress to the last four of the UEFA Champions League and secure a top four finish in the Barclays Premier League. Enjoy interviews with the men who have mattered and look back on some magical memories from the last twelve months in this year's official LFC Annual.

LFC Review of the 2007-08 season:

August:

Rafael Benitez's new-look Liverpool got their campaign off to a winning start as Steven Gerrard was the opening day hero with a sublime free-kick into the top corner of the Aston Villa net on a boiling hot afternoon in the Midlands. It was the ideal start to the season for the Reds, but disappointment was to follow just a week later. Liverpool dominated against Chelsea but had to settle for a draw after Frank Lampard took advantage of a crazy refereeing decision by Rob Styles to level from the spot after Fernando Torres had served notice of his intentions for the months ahead with a stunning individual goal. Sunderland were comfortably disposed of at the Stadium of Light - a game which saw Momo Sissoko grab his first goal for the Reds - whilst, more importantly, the Champions League qualifier with Toulouse was overcome with victories in both home and away legs.

September:

Kopites were singing about title challenges after a 6-0 demolition of Derby County at Anfield as the Reds ran riot against the newly promoted side. Ryan Babel - another new summer recruit - scored the pick of the goals whilst Fernando Torres was on target again to net his first goal at the Kop end. A goalless draw at Portsmouth followed just days before the first big Champions League clash of the season as Dirk Kuyt earned a point with a well directed header in Porto. If the season was to be remembered by the costly points dropped at Anfield, then Birmingham became the first 'smaller' side to leave Anfield with perhaps more than they should have done after Steve Bruce's side battled out a goalless draw, but the goals flowed three days later when the Reds got their Carling Cup campaign off to a winning start as Fernando Torres bagged a treble in a 4-2 thumping of Reading. The month ended with our first away win of the league season as Yossi Benayoun netted late on to secure all three points at Wigan.

October:

Liverpool's Champions League hopes were dented when Marseille came to Anfield and surprised everybody by silencing the Kop and heading back to France with all three points. There would be work to do for the Reds to qualify for the last sixteen. Further frustration followed when Tottenham also left Merseyside with a point to show for their efforts in an entertaining 2-2 draw - although it could have been much worse had our prolific Spanish striker not headed home an injury time equaliser. There's nothing like a good derby victory to get you back on track and although we did it the hard way after Sami Hyypia's early own goal at Goodison, Dirk Kuyt twice kept his nerve from the spot to ensure

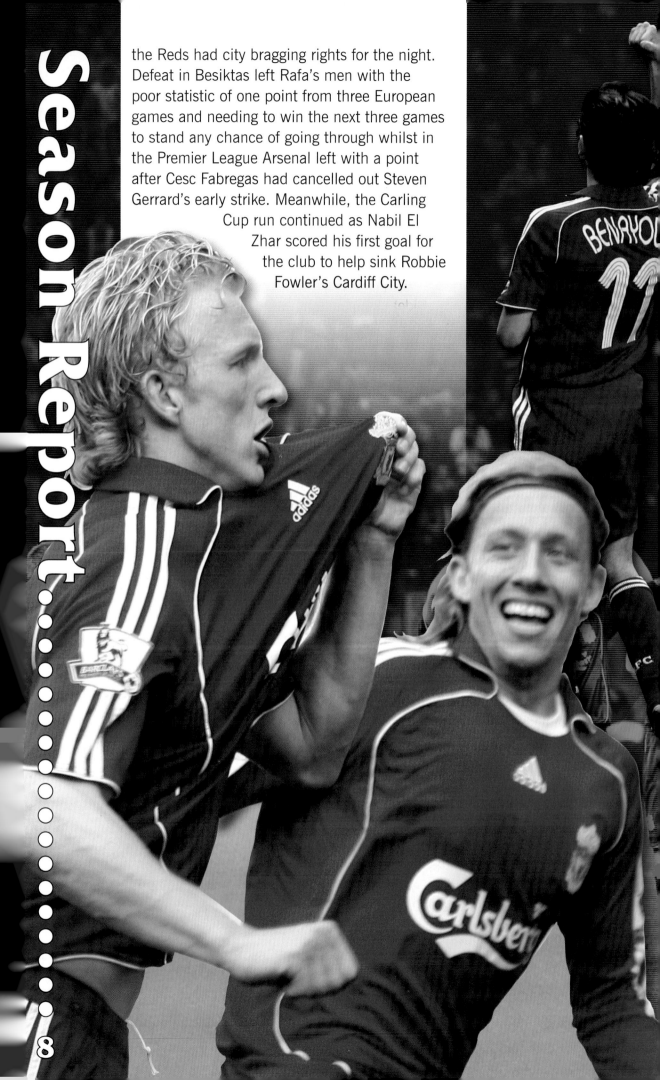

the Reds had city bragging rights for the night. Defeat in Besiktas left Rafa's men with the poor statistic of one point from three European games and needing to win the next three games to stand any chance of going through whilst in the Premier League Arsenal left with a point after Cesc Fabregas had cancelled out Steven Gerrard's early strike. Meanwhile, the Carling Cup run continued as Nabil El Zhar scored his first goal for the club to help sink Robbie Fowler's Cardiff City.

November:

A goalless draw with Blackburn got the month underway before the Reds set about the task of salvaging their European dreams - and did so in emphatic style with a record-breaking 8-0 demolition of Besiktas at Anfield, in which Yossi Benayoun chipped in with a hat-trick and both Peter Crouch and Ryan Babel netted twice. Liverpool had suddenly hit a winning streak and after Fernando Torres had seen off the challenge of Fulham at Anfield, the Reds tore Newcastle apart on their own pitch and ran out easy 3-0 winners. It was the ideal form in which to go into their next Champions League assignment - and the goals kept coming as Porto were demolished 4-1, leaving the Reds one away win in Marseille in their final group game away from qualification.

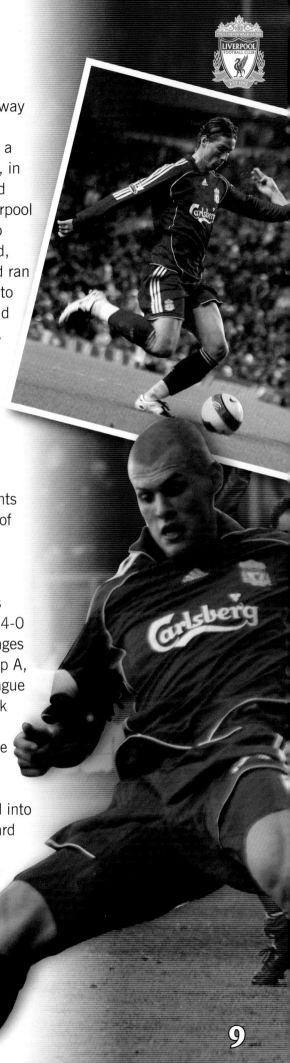

December:

Four goals from four different goalscorers sent Bolton packing at Anfield before arguably one of the low points of the season as the Reds suffered their first reversal of the league campaign - at relegation battling Reading. It was hardly the ideal warm-up for their French test in the Stade Velodrome, but the old mantra of never betting against Liverpool in Europe again rang true as Rafa Benitez's men turned on the style to chalk up a 4-0 victory and guarantee their place in the knock-out stages of the tournament. After a terrible start to life in Group A, it was now three wins in a row in the Champions League - and Inter Milan were to be next on the agenda. Back on home soil Carlos Tevez snatched three points for Manchester United at Anfield whilst our interest in the Carling Cup was ended with a 2-0 defeat at Chelsea. The Reds improved in time to give their fans an early Christmas present however, as four goals were rattled into the Portsmouth goal at Anfield and then Steven Gerrard netted a last minute Boxing Day winner at Pride Park to secure three precious points. Our final game of the year was one of the most one-sided matches of the previous twelve months - but Manchester City's defence stood firm in the face of relentless Reds pressure to steal a point from a goalless draw.

January:

If not the worst possible start to a new year, then perhaps the most unlikely one as Titus Bramble - that much-maligned defender - blasted an unstoppable shot into the Anfield Road net to earn a point for Wigan at Anfield. Not what we had in mind at all! It was to be the start of a frustrating run of draws with Luton holding their illustrious opposition to a 1-1 score in the FA Cup third round tie and then Middlesbrough achieving the same result at the Riverside - although Fernando Torres' strike to level the scores was one of the goals of the season. Thankfully normality was resumed in the Cup replay as Luton were on the end of a 5-0 hiding but it was to be a month full of goals and shocks from then on as Aston Villa took a point in a four goal thriller at Anfield and then Havant and Waterlooville, our FA Cup fourth round opponents from the Blue Square South division, shocked the footballing world by twice taking the lead only for Liverpool to eventually get going and run out 5-2 winners. An up and down month ended on a low note as Mark Noble slotted home a late penalty to send the Reds crashing to defeat at West Ham.

February:

Three second half goals at Anfield eventually saw off the challenge of Roy Keane's Sunderland before the trip to Chelsea when the Reds turned in one of their better displays at Stamford Bridge to earn a point. That morale boosting result counted for little the following week, however, when Liverpool's luck in the FA Cup finally ran out at the hands of Barnsley who turned the form book upside down to run out 2-1 winners at Anfield. If we couldn't beat Barnsley then what chance would we have beating Inter just a few days later as the 'Super Sixteen' phase of the Champions League got underway? We should have known better than to doubt the confidence of the players as they turned in yet another first class European display to carve out a two goal lead to take to the San Siro thanks to goals from Dirk Kuyt and Steven Gerrard. An Anfield thriller against Middlesbrough followed as Fernando Torres again bagged a hat-trick to secure the points in a 3-2 victory.

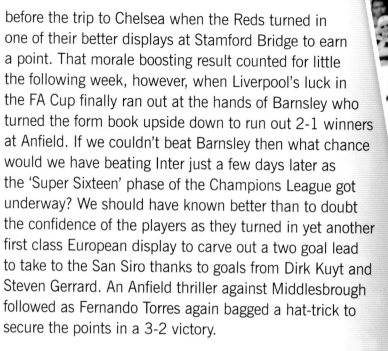

March:

Three league games kicked off the month and three wins were achieved with ten goals scored against Bolton, West Ham and Newcastle. Next up was the second leg in Italy and the question being asked was could we successfully defend our 2-0 lead? Few people predicted we'd actually go to the San Siro and win - but thanks to another strike from Fernando Torres that's exactly what happened. Liverpool again proved themselves the masters of European football to set up a quarter-final date with Arsenal. It was back down to earth with a bump, though, just a couple of weeks later when our chances to cut Manchester United's lead at the top of the table to just eight points were lost at Old Trafford after Javier Mascherano was dismissed by Steven Bennett for two bookable offences. United eventually ran out 3-0 winners to open up a 14 point gap and kill off any slight hopes we may have harboured of getting back into the title battle. The challenge now was to secure fourth place and with Everton hot on our heels,

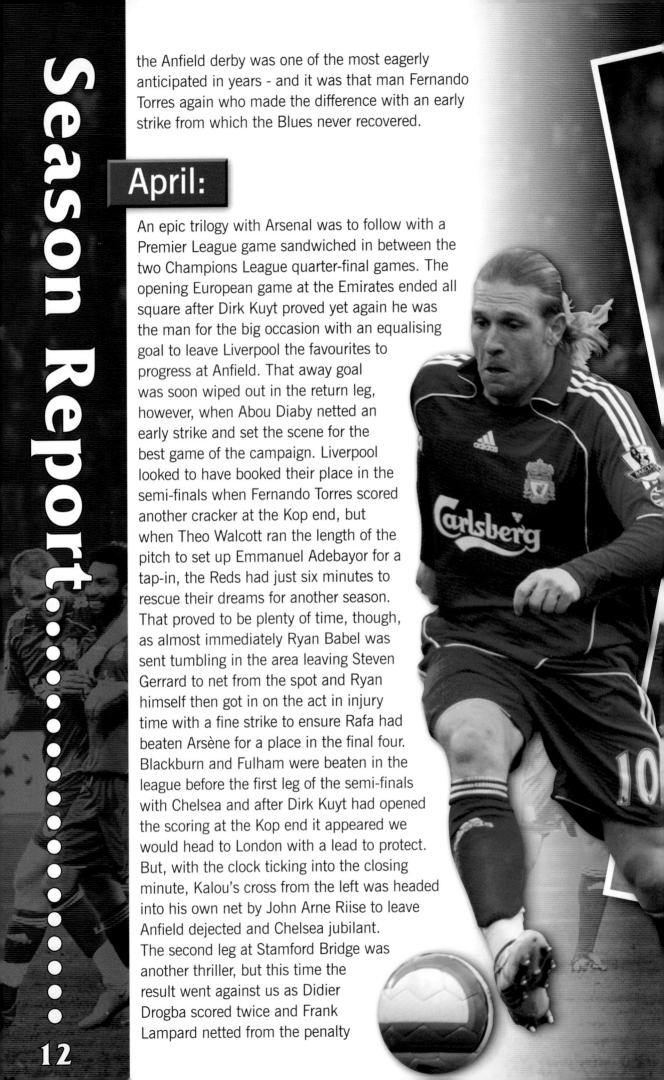

the Anfield derby was one of the most eagerly anticipated in years - and it was that man Fernando Torres again who made the difference with an early strike from which the Blues never recovered.

April:

An epic trilogy with Arsenal was to follow with a Premier League game sandwiched in between the two Champions League quarter-final games. The opening European game at the Emirates ended all square after Dirk Kuyt proved yet again he was the man for the big occasion with an equalising goal to leave Liverpool the favourites to progress at Anfield. That away goal was soon wiped out in the return leg, however, when Abou Diaby netted an early strike and set the scene for the best game of the campaign. Liverpool looked to have booked their place in the semi-finals when Fernando Torres scored another cracker at the Kop end, but when Theo Walcott ran the length of the pitch to set up Emmanuel Adebayor for a tap-in, the Reds had just six minutes to rescue their dreams for another season. That proved to be plenty of time, though, as almost immediately Ryan Babel was sent tumbling in the area leaving Steven Gerrard to net from the spot and Ryan himself then got in on the act in injury time with a fine strike to ensure Rafa had beaten Arsène for a place in the final four. Blackburn and Fulham were beaten in the league before the first leg of the semi-finals with Chelsea and after Dirk Kuyt had opened the scoring at the Kop end it appeared we would head to London with a lead to protect. But, with the clock ticking into the closing minute, Kalou's cross from the left was headed into his own net by John Arne Riise to leave Anfield dejected and Chelsea jubilant. The second leg at Stamford Bridge was another thriller, but this time the result went against us as Didier Drogba scored twice and Frank Lampard netted from the penalty

spot to eventually render goals from Fernando Torres and Ryan Babel meaningless as we crashed out 4-3 on aggregate.

May:

With fourth place in the league already secured, the final two matches of the season counted for little but Fernando Torres - who else? - ensured our final home game of the season was a winning one as he netted for the eighth game in a row in front of his own supporters. And then another record was sent tumbling on the final day as Fernando Torres was again on target in a 2-0 win at Tottenham to break Ruud van Nistelrooy's record for the most amount of goals scored by a foreigner in his debut season in English football.

Rafael Benitez – The Interview

Do you think your team has improved from last year?

Yes, I think so. The squad is better and we have a better team. Especially in the last three months; the understanding between the players was really good, we were winning games and scoring goals. We nearly got to the final of the Champions League.

Was Fernando Torres your number one target last summer?

Yes, we had a list of about 12 strikers and we were checking everything about them: the age, quality and price. At the end, Torres was the first target.

Did you see it as a gamble at all, because a few other clubs had looked at him but not made the move?

Not a gamble. In terms of the player, we knew. We had a lot of information and I'd spoken to him. From talking to Reina or Xabi, we knew he wanted to move to a top side, but for us £20million was a lot of money.

Did he take much persuading?

Not really. He was really pleased. I was on holiday the first time I spoke to him on the phone and he was walking his dog. We spoke for one or two minutes but later he told me he thought it was a joke. I needed to talk with him again and tell him it was true and that we needed to progress. I think in the end he was surprised.

What were the aims for you and your staff at the start of last season?

We always think about winning trophies. You don't say which ones. You want to score a lot of goals and win trophies. As soon as the season starts you say the Premier League and Champions League are the priorities, but if you progress in the FA Cup and maybe can't do anything in the League, the target is the FA Cup.

When did you first realise that Steven Gerrard and Fernando had struck up this really special bond?

We needed to find a balance. The team was attacking and conceding goals. We needed to control it and we could do that by using two holding midfielders with the power and strength of Gerrard going forward. As soon as we started playing like that, the understanding with Torres was easy.

The first home game saw Chelsea escape with a point after a really poor penalty decision...

Everyone could see it was a poor decision, especially Drogba. He was surprised. In a game against a top side it cost us two points and also confidence. We could have been higher in the table. You cannot control everything, we couldn't do anything. But we needed to keep going. We were much better than them, so that gave us confidence. We passed the ball really well and didn't give them many chances.

You then beat Derby 6-0 and were scoring a lot of goals. You went on to net 119 in all. Was there a change of mentality this season?

Not really. There were two or three things that happened: we conceded more goals from set pieces when we were doing the same things, and we scored more goals when we were doing the same things. You can't always explain. I think it's down to the quality of the players. We have better players, so we were attacking and creating more chances.

You scored more goals than Arsenal. Do you feel sometimes you don't get the credit you deserve for your attacking football?

When you talk about Arsenal, they play offensive and it's pretty. Everyone can say it's fantastic. For me, it's about winning trophies and to do this you must always have a balance between defence and attack. We think about clean sheets and scoring goals. I try to create a balance with a team that's strong at the back and also good in attack.

As the season progressed you began to draw more games. Is it these draws that ultimately cost you the title?

I think so. We lost a little bit of confidence because we were making mistakes and, without creating chances, the other teams were scoring. I remember two or three games: against Tottenham we had two or three chances after scoring, but then conceded two goals. This kind of game makes a massive difference in terms of confidence when you want to win the title.

With all these draws, the last thing you needed was a trip to Goodison but you ended up getting a last-minute penalty...

It was a good game. Everyone was talking about the substitution of Gerrard but I decided to introduce Lucas, whose final shot (seconds before the penalty) was really good. It was a penalty. Kuyt needed to be there and be brave, but he is a player you can trust. It was a fantastic day for us.

Yes, Dirk doesn't always grab the headlines like Fernando, but presumably you don't underestimate his contribution after what was a difficult summer for him, losing his father?

Kuyt has a fantastic mentality and a strong character. He is a winner, a fighter. He was determined to do something important after the summer. I think it's important our fans give credit to Kuyt. Here is a striker who scored a lot of goals in Holland, who came here and played as a second striker, who works really hard for the team but doesn't score as many goals, and then we decide to use him as a right winger. He has been fantastic and has scored important goals in important games. I am really pleased with him – he is a player you can always trust.

There was also a lot of things going on off the pitch, but you received tremendous support from the fans. Does it help you to do your job when you know you have the full backing of the supporters?

The supporters have been fantastic with me from the start. Before the Porto game (when fans marched outside Anfield) it was really important for the team and also for me. Always I say thank-you to the fans, and it's thanks to them that we progressed in the Champions League. They created a positive atmosphere for the team and supported them all the time. That was key.

It was a difficult season off the pitch. Did you ever tire of questions at every press conference about things you can't control?

Yes, but football is like this now. The journalists and fans need to ask questions. You need to be calm and find the right answers. I was at a dinner with fans and they were asking me why I only ever said three or four things. I said that it's important not to say too much because otherwise, after games, you could see a lot of headlines and then you are having to correct yourself. It's better not to say too much to the cameras, it's better for the team.

15

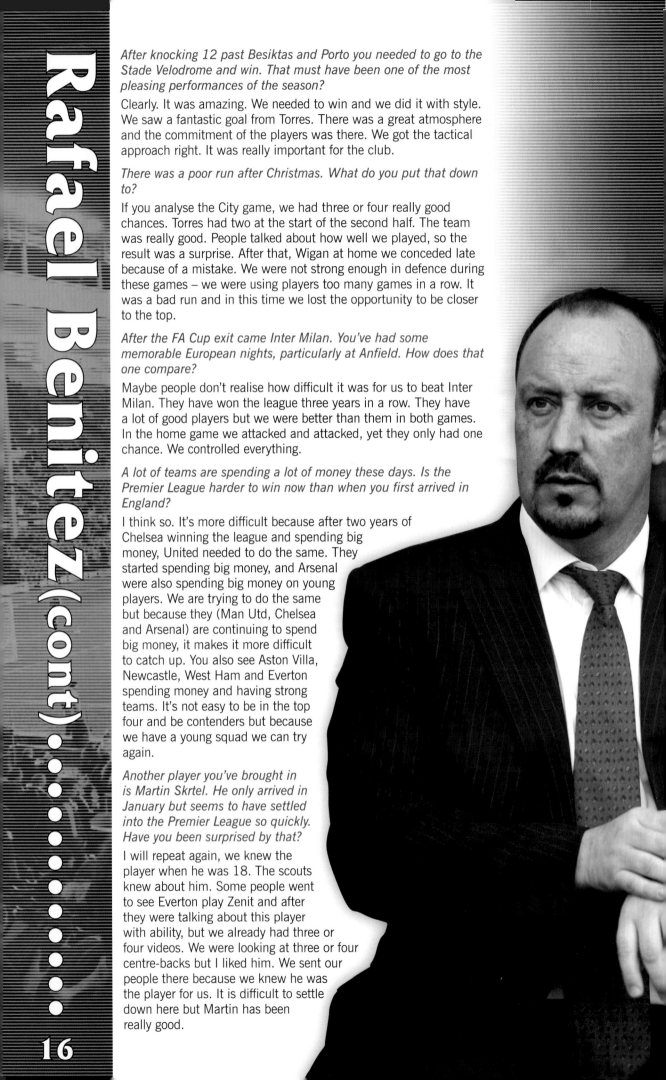

After knocking 12 past Besiktas and Porto you needed to go to the Stade Velodrome and win. That must have been one of the most pleasing performances of the season?

Clearly. It was amazing. We needed to win and we did it with style. We saw a fantastic goal from Torres. There was a great atmosphere and the commitment of the players was there. We got the tactical approach right. It was really important for the club.

There was a poor run after Christmas. What do you put that down to?

If you analyse the City game, we had three or four really good chances. Torres had two at the start of the second half. The team was really good. People talked about how well we played, so the result was a surprise. After that, Wigan at home we conceded late because of a mistake. We were not strong enough in defence during these games – we were using players too many games in a row. It was a bad run and in this time we lost the opportunity to be closer to the top.

After the FA Cup exit came Inter Milan. You've had some memorable European nights, particularly at Anfield. How does that one compare?

Maybe people don't realise how difficult it was for us to beat Inter Milan. They have won the league three years in a row. They have a lot of good players but we were better than them in both games. In the home game we attacked and attacked, yet they only had one chance. We controlled everything.

A lot of teams are spending a lot of money these days. Is the Premier League harder to win now than when you first arrived in England?

I think so. It's more difficult because after two years of Chelsea winning the league and spending big money, United needed to do the same. They started spending big money, and Arsenal were also spending big money on young players. We are trying to do the same but because they (Man Utd, Chelsea and Arsenal) are continuing to spend big money, it makes it more difficult to catch up. You also see Aston Villa, Newcastle, West Ham and Everton spending money and having strong teams. It's not easy to be in the top four and be contenders but because we have a young squad we can try again.

Another player you've brought in is Martin Skrtel. He only arrived in January but seems to have settled into the Premier League so quickly. Have you been surprised by that?

I will repeat again, we knew the player when he was 18. The scouts knew about him. Some people went to see Everton play Zenit and after they were talking about this player with ability, but we already had three or four videos. We were looking at three or four centre-backs but I liked him. We sent our people there because we knew he was the player for us. It is difficult to settle down here but Martin has been really good.

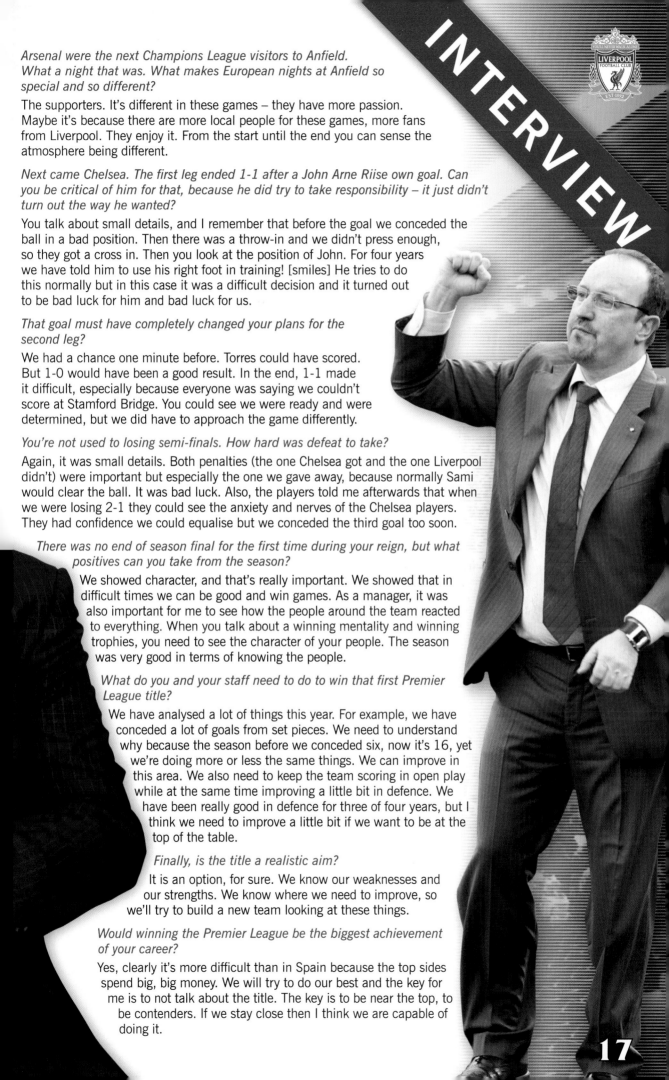

Arsenal were the next Champions League visitors to Anfield. What a night that was. What makes European nights at Anfield so special and so different?

The supporters. It's different in these games – they have more passion. Maybe it's because there are more local people for these games, more fans from Liverpool. They enjoy it. From the start until the end you can sense the atmosphere being different.

Next came Chelsea. The first leg ended 1-1 after a John Arne Riise own goal. Can you be critical of him for that, because he did try to take responsibility – it just didn't turn out the way he wanted?

You talk about small details, and I remember that before the goal we conceded the ball in a bad position. Then there was a throw-in and we didn't press enough, so they got a cross in. Then you look at the position of John. For four years we have told him to use his right foot in training! [smiles] He tries to do this normally but in this case it was a difficult decision and it turned out to be bad luck for him and bad luck for us.

That goal must have completely changed your plans for the second leg?

We had a chance one minute before. Torres could have scored. But 1-0 would have been a good result. In the end, 1-1 made it difficult, especially because everyone was saying we couldn't score at Stamford Bridge. You could see we were ready and were determined, but we did have to approach the game differently.

You're not used to losing semi-finals. How hard was defeat to take?

Again, it was small details. Both penalties (the one Chelsea got and the one Liverpool didn't) were important but especially the one we gave away, because normally Sami would clear the ball. It was bad luck. Also, the players told me afterwards that when we were losing 2-1 they could see the anxiety and nerves of the Chelsea players. They had confidence we could equalise but we conceded the third goal too soon.

There was no end of season final for the first time during your reign, but what positives can you take from the season?

We showed character, and that's really important. We showed that in difficult times we can be good and win games. As a manager, it was also important for me to see how the people around the team reacted to everything. When you talk about a winning mentality and winning trophies, you need to see the character of your people. The season was very good in terms of knowing the people.

What do you and your staff need to do to win that first Premier League title?

We have analysed a lot of things this year. For example, we have conceded a lot of goals from set pieces. We need to understand why because the season before we conceded six, now it's 16, yet we're doing more or less the same things. We can improve in this area. We also need to keep the team scoring in open play while at the same time improving a little bit in defence. We have been really good in defence for three of four years, but I think we need to improve a little bit if we want to be at the top of the table.

Finally, is the title a realistic aim?

It is an option, for sure. We know our weaknesses and our strengths. We know where we need to improve, so we'll try to build a new team looking at these things.

Would winning the Premier League be the biggest achievement of your career?

Yes, clearly it's more difficult than in Spain because the top sides spend big, big money. We will try to do our best and the key for me is to not talk about the title. The key is to be near the top, to be contenders. If we stay close then I think we are capable of doing it.

Spot the difference..........

Study the picture below closely then use your skill
to spot where you think the ball might be.
The solution is on page 61.

Spot the ball.....................

Steven Gerrard – The Interview

How will you look back on 2007-08, Steven?

I went on record recently and said that I have to be proud of my teammates even though we fell away in the title race. We can be really proud of reaching the last four in the Champions League – another great run in Europe – and getting a top four finish in a really tough league. But there is still some improvement needed.

We were top of the league in September – everyone thought we were going to push on. Is there a game or period you can identify when the title challenge slipped away?

Yes, silly results against teams we should be beating. Look at Reading away, where we were beaten 3-1. There were a couple of silly draws at home against sides you need to perform perfectly against and take maximum points from. You can get involved in the title race and even win it without beating the top three home and away. You don't have to take maximum points from them if you perform perfectly against the others, but we haven't done that. We've dropped stupid points.

Our form in latter months has been as good as if not better than the top two – is that frustrating in a way?

Yes, it is because we know we are capable of going on consistent runs and beating anyone. We started off that way, expectations were high and players were making the right noises. We thought this year we were going to be a lot closer, so now we need to learn from our mistakes – as we keep saying.

Your away form was great last season – is that down to a change in mentality?

Yes, maybe. But also the manager has signed winners, players with a good mentality. That has shown away from home where we've been really hard to beat. Players have performed really well, the likes of your Leivas and Mascheranos. They are good players to have away from home – they dig in and do a lot of work that goes unnoticed. But we also expect good results at home, and that's what's disappointing when you look at the Wigan and Aston Villa results.

What was your personal highlight of the season?

I don't really look back on individual things. Obviously I'm happy with all my goals – to get 21 is a good achievement for myself but I'm more interested in where we finish in the league and how we do in the cups.

Steven Gerrard Facts

Date of birth:
30 May 1980

Place of birth:
Whiston, England

Height:
6 ft 0 in (1.83 m)

Playing position:
Midfielder

Playing number:
8

You mention 21 goals – is that about the target you set yourself?

It wasn't, if I'm honest. Maybe five or six years ago it was good if a midfielder got into double figures, but the likes of Paul Scholes and Frank Lampard took it to another level by getting 15-plus. So, to get more than 20 goals is really good. I try to get as many as I can and the target is always double figures. Maybe I've got into the 20s because I've played further forward for quite a few games.

What about the low point?

When we've lost or drawn games we should have won, then looked at the gap to the top and seen it sliding away. That's the disappointing thing because my expectations at the start of the season were high. I thought we would have been involved in a title race come March or April but unfortunately we were out of it.

People will look back on your stats and say last season was one of your best from a personal point of view: 21 goals, countless assists, making your 400th appearance. How satisfied were you with your own form?

To be honest, I felt coming out of pre-season perhaps the best I've felt. I had a good rest and felt like I was flying going into the Villa game. My performances against Villa and Chelsea were good but then I broke my toe, which set me back for four to six weeks. Since then I think I've performed consistently.

Steven Gerrard (cont) ··········

It's also been a year when you've developed this incredible partnership with Fernando. How do you feel when you hear people comparing it to watching Ian Rush and Kenny Dalglish?

It's really flattering because they are two legends at the club. Kenny Dalglish and Ian Rush! They are two people me and Fernando look up to – everyone at the club does. To be talked about in the same breath is flattering but they did it for many, many years. Their partnership was also successful in that they had trophies to back it up, and that's my and Fernando's aim.

As an onlooker, it appears similar to the relationship you had with another great striker, Michael Owen – almost telepathic at times. Is that how it feels?

It does when I set him up and he scores. I still get the same buzz and the same feeling. I used to set Michael up from midfield, whereas I'm a lot closer to Fernando on the pitch. It's a little bit easier because of that, and also his movement and runs are fantastic. I enjoy playing with him, it's great to have him here and he's been Player of the Year hands down. Hopefully he can take this into next season.

Can you remember a foreign player having the kind of impact Fernando has in his first season?

No, not really. But if you look at players like Sami Hyypiä - he made the same level of impact but Fernando will get all the plaudits because of the goals and the fact he's winning football matches for us.

How far away are we from a title challenge - is it just about one or two world-class additions?

It's difficult to say how many world-class players. You look at the points difference and over the last few years we have made it smaller. Playing against your Arsenals and Chelseas, it has been close. We are giving them good games which are tight and get decided on small details. If we can make the team a little bit stronger, have a few more options and match-winners, and make the team a tiny bit better defensively, we can do it.

The spine of this team, with Pepe, Jamie, Javier, yourself and Fernando - that's as good as anything in the world, isn't it?

In my opinion, yes. If you look at the quality we have down the spine, it is fantastic. We have other good players as well, though.

22

Youngsters such as Ryan Babel, Lucas and Martin Skrtel now have a year in English football behind them – how big a factor could that be next season? Do you expect even bigger things from them?

The experience will certainly help. I remember when I was a young kid playing in Europe and making mistakes – all that experience helps you become a better player. The likes of Lucas and Ryan will benefit from the amount of football they have been given this season.

How confident are you of mounting a serious title challenge in 2008-09?

Obviously I have to be careful that I don't send expectations through the roof again, but for me I am desperate for it. I believe in this team and this manager, and believe we can make it happen. We need help and new players, and the manager needs help from the board to make these signings happen and make us stronger. I do expect us to be involved next season.

Three English teams in the Champions League semis last season - is winning the title now tougher than it's ever been?

It is tough, that's what people have to realise. We are strengthening all the time, working as hard as any other team and having as many shots on goal. Sometimes you have to realise there are other sides that are as good as us who are strengthening and working hard as well. They want it just as much as us. But it has been a long time for this club (winning the league), so we all maybe need to give that extra five or 10 per cent.

How happy are you at Liverpool?

Well, I'm happy. I am enjoying my football. Obviously I am not happy ending the season without a trophy because I am a winner and that's what I play the game for. I like finishing the season and having a trophy or cup final to look back on and seeing I've achieved something. The experiences I've had at this club in Istanbul, Cardiff, Super Cup finals and the Carling Cup – I want these again because I've enjoyed them so much.

Sami Hyypiä - A 10-year tribute

Sami Hyypiä may be entering the twilight of his career at the very highest level, but Rafael Benitez didn't hesitate to offer him a new one year deal and a chance to take a glorious Liverpool career into a tenth season.

The Finnish international - arguably the club's best pound for pound signing in recent history - will complete a decade of service at Anfield this season and admits the chance to prolong his stay on Merseyside was far too good an opportunity to refuse.

"I'm delighted that everyone wants me to stay here," he said after penning his new deal. "I have a good relationship with everyone at the club, the fans and the players, so it would have been a big wrench for me to leave.

"But I wasn't thinking about it too much. The most important thing for me was to concentrate on the games and if I played well then maybe the club would want me to stay.

"I would have had some options to go elsewhere but everything here has been great and I have enjoyed everything about my time here.

"It's not so common for a foreign player in this country to spend ten years at one club so I am delighted to stay with this great club.

"We will see what next year brings. I will keep working hard and keep myself fit and whenever the manager needs me I will be there."

Sami Hyypiä was certainly needed more than many would have thought last season as an injury to Daniel Agger opened the door for big Sami to play a crucial role in the Reds' quest for domestic and European glory.

"It makes me feel good that I'm still here after nine years. It shows I've done something right," he added.

"Of course it's unfortunate that Daniel was out for the season, but because of that I've played a lot more than I thought I would, and of course I've enjoyed every minute of it."

Sami Hyypiä's admirers stretch far and wide away from Anfield, but within the club special words are reserved for a man who made his 300th appearance for the Reds last season.

Sami Hyypiä Facts

Date of birth:
7 October 1973

Place of birth:
Porvoo, Finland

Height:
6 ft 4 in (1.93 m)

Playing position:
Centre Back

Playing number:
4

"I've been saying it for years, Sami will go down in history alongside the likes of Ron Yeats, Alan Hansen and Emlyn Hughes," said fellow centre back Jamie Carragher.

"When you think of the foreign players who have played in this country, for me Sami is up there with Dennis Bergkamp and Gianfranco Zola.

"Not many players have come to the Premiership from abroad and played for just one club for as long as Sami has and in all the time he's been at Liverpool you could probably count his bad performances on the fingers of one hand.

"Sami is a top class professional and that's why he's still been able to perform as well as he has been doing even at 34," said Carragher.

"There was a spell when the critics were looking at his performances and maybe getting on his back a bit but, when it comes down to it, it is difficult for anyone to play well when the team isn't playing well.

"You are always learning in football and you try to take things from all the players you work with.

"In Sami's case the thing that has always impressed me most is the way he looks after himself.

"He's never carried much weight or anything like that.

"Even when he was on the fringes of the team he never let his fitness levels drop and that can be a difficult time for someone who has been first choice for so long.

"It's that kind of professionalism which has allowed Sami to play at the top level for so long and hopefully he'll be there for some time to come as well."

Manager Rafael Benitez is equally as fulsome in his praise for the long-serving Finn.

He said: "Sami is a fantastic person, a very good professional and a very good player.

"When he was playing too many games in a row he was a bit tired and that affected him.

"We had a few players in defence who were injured so we could not change him and give him the rest that we wanted to give him.

"He was also playing a lot of games with the national team and then coming back here and playing games for us – at 34 years of age this is not easy and it was not easy for him.

Fernando Torres – The Interview

If you've been on the Kop over the past year then the words will be familiar by now….

His armband proved he was a red Torres Torres

You'll Never Walk Alone it said Torres Torres

We bought the lad from sunny Spain

He gets the ball and scores again

Fer-nan-do Torres Liverpool's number nine

The Kop has been bouncing like never before to the tune of the Reds' record signing as goal after goal went in at Anfield during the most remarkable debut season English football has seen for many, many years.

Records were sent tumbling almost on a weekly basis as Torres finished his first campaign in the Premier League with 33 goals, including 24 in the league which saw him surpass Ruud van Nistelrooy for the greatest goalscoring season in a debut season by a foreigner. He also ended the campaign having netted in eight successive home games - equalling another club record. And, just for good measure, he also became the first Liverpool player to net 20 goals since the days of Robbie Fowler.

If all that was needed to mould a title challenging team was a goalscorer extraordinaire then Rafael Benitez has found his man.

Superlatives have been trotted out by the fans game after game following another Torres masterclass - but the man himself has remained humble despite seeing his reputation soar over the past year.

Fernando Torres Facts

Date of birth:
20 March 1984

Place of birth:
Madrid, Spain

Height:
6 ft 1 in (1.85 m)

Playing position:
Striker

Playing number:
9

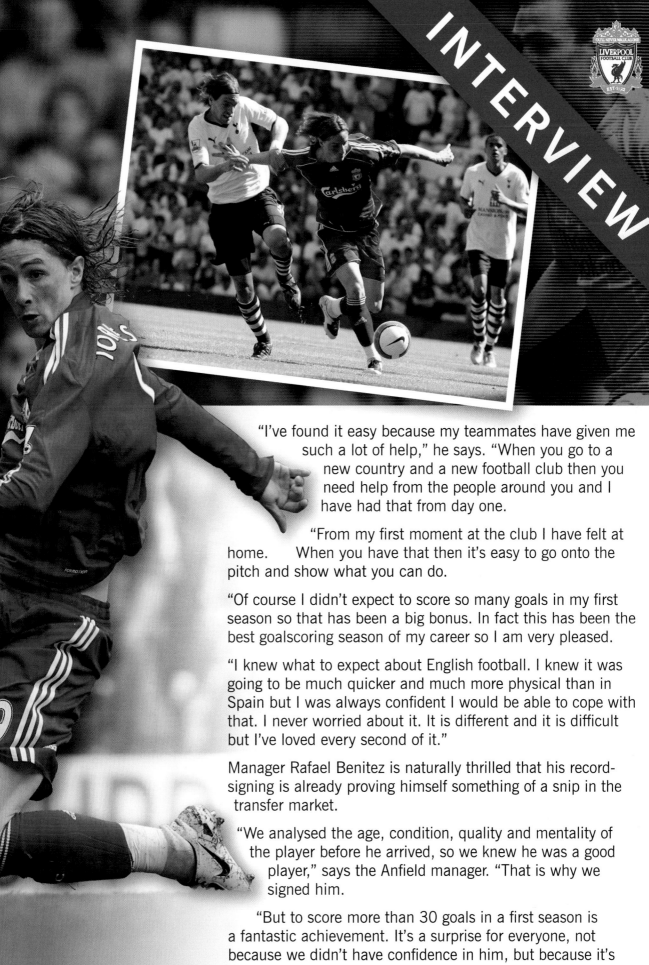

"I've found it easy because my teammates have given me such a lot of help," he says. "When you go to a new country and a new football club then you need help from the people around you and I have had that from day one.

"From my first moment at the club I have felt at home. When you have that then it's easy to go onto the pitch and show what you can do.

"Of course I didn't expect to score so many goals in my first season so that has been a big bonus. In fact this has been the best goalscoring season of my career so I am very pleased.

"I knew what to expect about English football. I knew it was going to be much quicker and much more physical than in Spain but I was always confident I would be able to cope with that. I never worried about it. It is different and it is difficult but I've loved every second of it."

Manager Rafael Benitez is naturally thrilled that his record-signing is already proving himself something of a snip in the transfer market.

"We analysed the age, condition, quality and mentality of the player before he arrived, so we knew he was a good player," says the Anfield manager. "That is why we signed him.

"But to score more than 30 goals in a first season is a fantastic achievement. It's a surprise for everyone, not because we didn't have confidence in him, but because it's his first year in the Premier League.

"I don't know why so many of his league goals have come at Anfield though. For me, it's a surprise because I'd have thought he'd score more goals away because of his pace and he'd get more space and it'd be easier for him.

"Maybe it's just a coincidence. But the motivation at Anfield is fantastic because of our supporters.

"He's scored at Stamford Bridge and the San Siro in the Champions League, so he has shown he can score anywhere."

Fernando's rapport with the fans has been a love affair gathering pace since he flew past Chelsea's Tal Ben Haim to net his first goal of the season against Chelsea at Anfield.

"Our fans are the best," he said. "They have given me great support but then they have been right behind the players through every game. Liverpool is like a family and it's great for me to be part of it.

"Of course the European nights have been special and hopefully there are many more to come. After the Arsenal game at Anfield the crowd was so loud that I was almost in tears. It was an incredible atmosphere.

"I'm proud they enjoy singing their song about me and it feels great on a matchday to know they are doing that for me. It also makes my family and friends proud because they know I am having such a good time at Liverpool and that I'm in a great place for my career.

"It's very important for me to make the

fans happy. We play football to give them enjoyment. I think they love me and I love them. It's great when kids and their grandads come up to me in the street and say 'you're the best'.

"I was with Kenny Dalglish the other day and you could see in the faces of the people how much of a hero he is, 20 years after he finished his career. I want everyone to remember me in 20 years time."

Such has been the impact made by Fernando Torres already, some fans are comparing him to legends from Anfield's glorious past - but he insists those comparisons are premature.

"I'm very proud but now is not the moment. Kenny, Robbie and Stevie [Gerrard] have a lot of trophies, a lot of titles and they have played hundreds of games for the club. They have been legends for lots of years," he added.

"This is only my first season at Liverpool and I want to play better for many more seasons yet. So far I've had one good season but Kenny and Robbie have had six, seven, eight or ten good seasons at Liverpool. It's different.

"When I have finished my career then maybe that will be the moment to talk about these things but not now. It's too early. It's important to me that the fans think highly of me and if they're saying these things then I would say 'thank you, but not yet'."

And asked if he would like to remain a Liverpool player for the rest of his career, he replied: "I hope so. I feel very confident here. If we can win trophies, then much better. This is my team, my city and Anfield is my pitch. I feel very good."

Quiz answers on page 60

02. Against which side did Ryan Babel score his first Liverpool goal?

03. Who returned to the coaching staff at the end of last season as assistant manager?

04. And who did he replace in that role?

05. How many goals did Steven Gerrard score last season?

06. Against which side did Fernando Torres score his first hat-trick for the Reds?

07. What number does Daniel Agger wear at Anfield?

08. What nationality is Lucas Leiva?

09. How many games did Liverpool lose in the Premier League last season?

10. Who scored an own goal in the Champions League semi-final first leg clash at Anfield?

11. What was the overall aggregate score in the
tie after the second leg?

12. Who wears the number 20 shirt at the club?

13. And which country does this player come
from?

14. Which side knocked us out of the FA Cup
last season?

15. Who scored for Liverpool in that game?

16. How many players did we have representing
us in the Spanish squad at Euro 2008?

17. Who is the manager of the Liverpool
reserve side?

18. Where did Liverpool's reserves play
their home games last season?

19. What is Liverpool's training ground called?

20. How many goals did Fernando Torres score
in his first season in England?

With Liverpool being top scorers in English football last season it's little wonder the 'Goal of the Season' competition on the club's official website was a close contest. After thousands of votes were cast from fans all over the world, here are your top ten strikes from our last campaign.

Goal 1: Fernando Torres v Marseille – 11 December 2007

Fernando Torres scored enough goals during his debut campaign to run his own Goal of the Season competition, but his strike in the intimidating arena of Marseille's Stade Velodrome not only kept Liverpool's European dreams alive - it was voted the Reds' best of 2007-08. Collecting the ball on the left side of the area, the in-form Spaniard made his way slalom-like through the heart of the French back-line - leaving defenders trailing in his wake before slotting the ball confidently and comfortably into the far corner of the net. The goal doubled Liverpool's lead on the night and put them within sight of the last sixteen of the competition.

Goal 2: Fernando Torres v Chelsea – 19 August 2007

How do you convince your new fans you are worth the record-breaking transfer fee the manager has splashed out on you during the summer? Score a wonder goal against one of your title rivals on your Anfield debut, that's how! Fernando Torres may have wondered how quickly he would prove himself in English football - he needn't have worried. From the moment he left Chelsea's Tal Ben Haim in a state of disbelief as he glided past him inside the area before stroking the ball past Petr Cech, he was well on his way towards becoming a Kop idol.

Goal 3: Steven Gerrard v Aston Villa – 11 August 2007

Liverpool were heading towards an undeserved opening day draw at Aston Villa after Gareth Barry had brought the home side into the game with an undeserved equaliser just six minutes from time. But when you have Steven Gerrard in your side there is no such thing as a lost cause and the fact was proved again as the skipper secured a brilliant victory with a last-gasp long range free kick which he curled high over the wall and into the roof of the net.

Goal 4: Steven Gerrard v Newcastle – 24 November 2007

It was another masterclass in the art of free-kick taking from the Liverpool captain as he put the Reds on course for an impressive victory at the home of struggling Newcastle.

Responding to the jeers of the Newcastle fans who held him partly responsible for a sub-standard England display just days before - Gerrard smashed home the opening goal of the game with a blistering long range strike which Shay Given simply waved goodbye as it fizzed past him into the goal.

Goal 5: Fernando Torres v Newcastle – 8 March 2008

The telepathy between Steven Gerrard and Fernando Torres was again evident for all to see as the Anfield duo combined to deadly effect against the Geordies. Having gathered the ball under control down the left side, Gerrard instantly drove a pass into Fernando's path and the Spaniard succeeded where Pele once failed by dummying the goalkeeper and then slotting the ball into an unguarded net. Quite simply the stuff of genius.

Goal 6: Ryan Babel v Derby County – 1 September 2007

In one of the most one-sided league matches played at Anfield in many a long year, new Dutch recruit Ryan Babel scored arguably the pick of the goals in the Reds' 6-0 win. Alvaro Arbeloa found space down the left to cut a perfect pass into Babel's path, and the flying winger made no mistake as he bypassed the challenges of two Derby players before firing the ball hard and true into the back of the Anfield Road net.

Goal 7: Fabio Aurelio v Bolton – 2 March 2008

The Brazilian full-back had been getting closer and closer to his first ever Liverpool goal with a number of 'close-calls' from dead ball situations - but his deadlock breaking strike was well worth waiting for. With Liverpool already ahead at the Reebok Stadium, Aurelio controlled the ball on his chest outside the area before volleying home a spectacular left footed shot which dipped into the far corner of the net. Let's hope we don't have as long a wait again before his next goal arrives…

Goal 8: Nabil El Zhar v Cardiff City – 31 October 2007

It may have 'only' been the Carling Cup - but try telling that to Moroccan youngster Nabil El Zhar who celebrated being given a rare chance to impress with a stunning goal at the Kop end. With Cardiff frustrating the Reds, it looked like it could be a frustrating night's work for Rafa's men, but El Zhar soon calmed any nerves of a Cup upset with a blistering long range drive which nestled in the right hand corner of the goal. Quality strike.

Goal 9: Fernando Torres v Derby County – 26 December 2007

It was El Nino's first goal in the league away from Anfield - but it was well worth waiting for. Relegation battling Derby were proving a tough nut to crack at Pride Park, but Torres soon broke their resistance with a trademark run, drop of the shoulder and clever nutmeg before creating the space to drill home a glorious left footed shot beyond the bewildered goalkeeper.

Goal 10: Fernando Torres v Fulham – 10 November 2007

It was route one from Liverpool - played to devastating effect. With the clock running down and the home side in danger of letting points slip away, goalkeeper Pepe Reina hammered the ball forward towards the chest of Fernando Torres. The Reds' striker got the ball under control and was soon one-on-one with the last man. One cut inside and left foot shot later and Fulham's resistance had finally been broken.

Ryan Babel – Profile

Ryan Babel has enjoyed settling into English football over the past year - but now he plans to take the Premier League by storm.

The Dutch star saw a cruel injury rob him of the chance to represent his country during Euro 2008 - but having worked his way back to full fitness, he's now ready to show why Rafael Benitez was so keen to spend so heavily on him twelve months ago.

"I definitely feel as though I got better as the season went on and I was much happier with my form in the second half of the season than in the first part," he said.

"The season went by really quickly but I am satisfied and it was very enjoyable. There were good moments and bad moments, happy times and sad times, but that's football.

"Next season I want to develop more, train even better, work even harder and look to improve more. I set myself a target of ten goals at the start of the season and I reached that which is very pleasing.

"There is still much more to come from me though. I think I will be a lot more settled next year because it's normal that you have to get used to things in your first season. For example, I have only recently moved into my new house so that's something I don't need to think about anymore. I can be completely settled next season and concentrate solely on football."

Many fans are excited by the rich potential of Ryan Babel and feel he could develop into one of the most exciting wide players in the game.

It's a view shared by those in and around the club as well.

Anfield legend Ian Rush said: "I think we'll be looking for him to get more involved next season and play more games. When he runs at defences he's direct and he's a menace. He's big and strong and we'll see progress from Babel if he's back fully fit.

"He's had a year now in the Premier League and he knows what it's all about, so hopefully he'll keep getting better."

And skipper Steven Gerrard is relishing the prospect of linking up with a player who now understands what English football is all about.

Ryan Babel Facts

Date of birth:
19 December 1986

Place of birth:
Amsterdam, Netherlands

Height:
6 ft 1 in (1.85 m)

Playing position:
Winger, Striker

Playing number:
19

"He's young and he's made a big impact from the bench, and he's done well in some matches he's started," he said. "He's got a bright future. If he's willing to learn then he's got the right players around him to help his game. It's all about Ryan now and how much he wants to take his game to the next level, because he's certainly got the attributes.

"Ryan has got the ability, there's no doubt about it. He's strong, quick, can set goals up and score. He's got it all. I've seen it with so many players when they've had this ability and not taken it to the next level. It's up to Ryan now how much he wants to be one of the top players about, because he certainly could be."

Gary Ablett – The Interview

Despite taking a hat-trick of trophies to Anfield last season, Gary Ablett has insisted there's room for improvement from his reserve team this year.

The young Reds landed the Reserve League North title at the end of an impressive campaign before securing the National title with victory over Aston Villa at Anfield.

With the Dallas Cup also added to the trophy haul for the season Ablett could be forgiven for praising his players for a perfect year - but he still wants more.

"I would probably give them seven and a half out of ten for the season," he reflected. "Maybe that's slightly cruel on them given the season they've had but I can see a lot more potential to come from some of them. Hopefully next season they can fulfil that potential and break into the first team.

"There is always room for improvement. We know we have good young players who are on different levels of the learning curve.

"It was a good season and we achieved what we wanted to achieve in terms of winning trophies, but I want to see more of them playing more first team games. We've had Insua and Plessis play for the first team towards the end of the season but the challenge is for the others to also make the breakthrough."

Insua impressed at full back towards the end of last season and Ablett has laid down the challenge for the Argentine youngster to make more progress this season.

"He's made a lot of progress, as have the majority of our young players. If you had said to me at the start of the season that we would have sent eight, nine or ten of the senior reserve players out on loan and that I'd have to cope with the young group that have just come in, I'd have thought we would struggle," he added.

"But credit to the younger group, they've knuckled down and tried to take on board what we have tried to teach them and we've reaped the benefits from that."

Perhaps the standout performer from the Reds' success at reserve level last season was Hungarian frontman Krisztian Nemeth - who led the scoring charts and was perhaps unfortunate not to enjoy a taste of first team action himself.

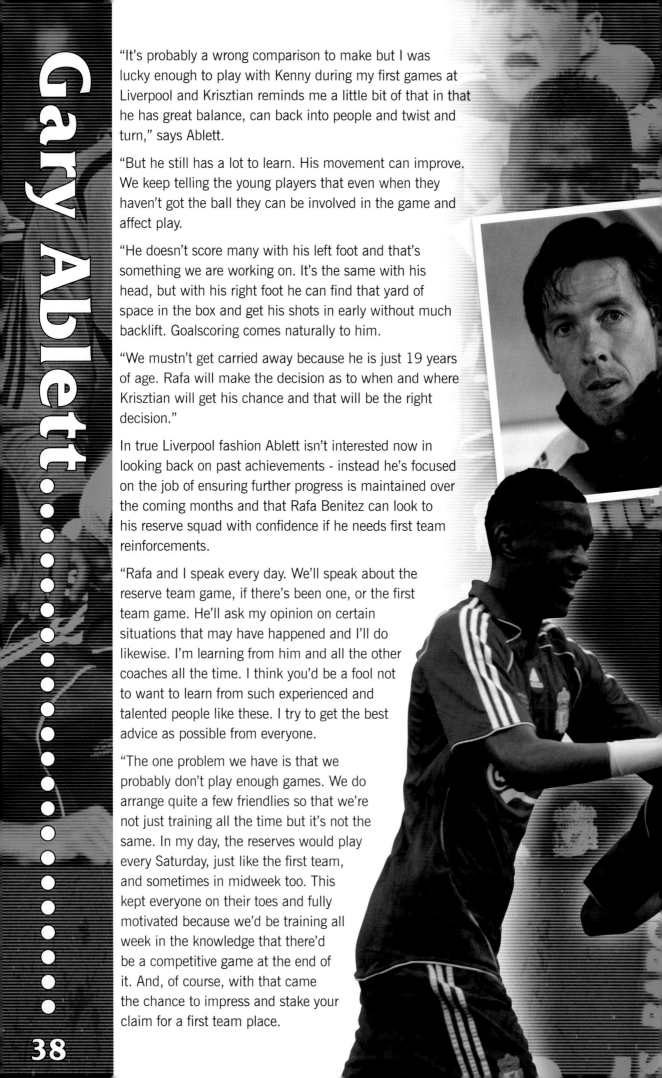

Gary Ablett

"It's probably a wrong comparison to make but I was lucky enough to play with Kenny during my first games at Liverpool and Krisztian reminds me a little bit of that in that he has great balance, can back into people and twist and turn," says Ablett.

"But he still has a lot to learn. His movement can improve. We keep telling the young players that even when they haven't got the ball they can be involved in the game and affect play.

"He doesn't score many with his left foot and that's something we are working on. It's the same with his head, but with his right foot he can find that yard of space in the box and get his shots in early without much backlift. Goalscoring comes naturally to him.

"We mustn't get carried away because he is just 19 years of age. Rafa will make the decision as to when and where Krisztian will get his chance and that will be the right decision."

In true Liverpool fashion Ablett isn't interested now in looking back on past achievements - instead he's focused on the job of ensuring further progress is maintained over the coming months and that Rafa Benitez can look to his reserve squad with confidence if he needs first team reinforcements.

"Rafa and I speak every day. We'll speak about the reserve team game, if there's been one, or the first team game. He'll ask my opinion on certain situations that may have happened and I'll do likewise. I'm learning from him and all the other coaches all the time. I think you'd be a fool not to want to learn from such experienced and talented people like these. I try to get the best advice as possible from everyone.

"The one problem we have is that we probably don't play enough games. We do arrange quite a few friendlies so that we're not just training all the time but it's not the same. In my day, the reserves would play every Saturday, just like the first team, and sometimes in midweek too. This kept everyone on their toes and fully motivated because we'd be training all week in the knowledge that there'd be a competitive game at the end of it. And, of course, with that came the chance to impress and stake your claim for a first team place.

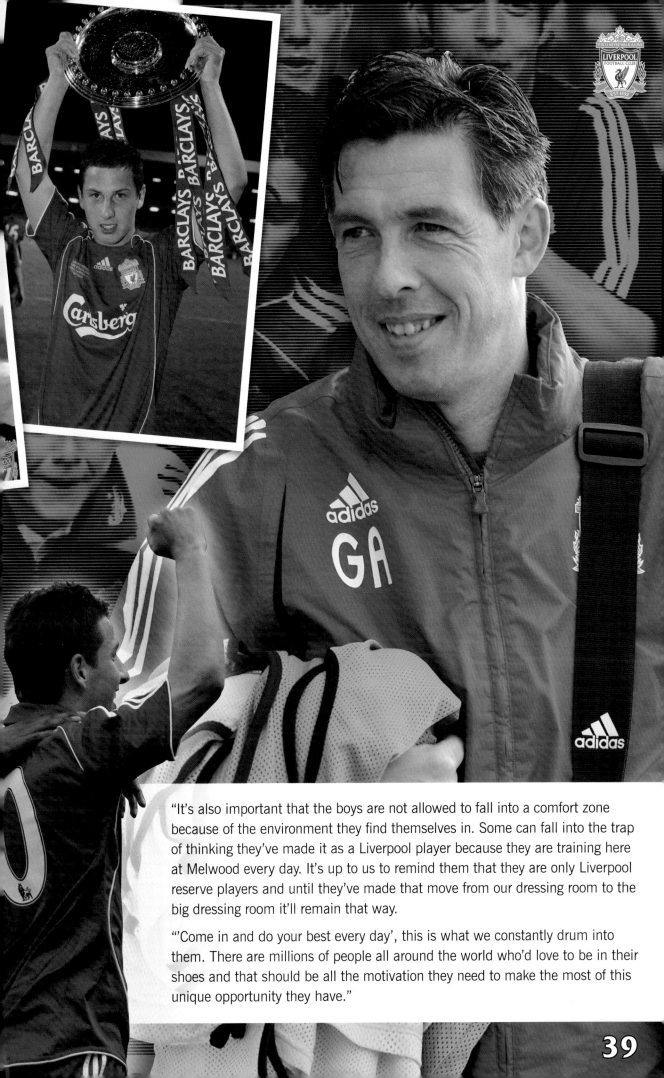

"It's also important that the boys are not allowed to fall into a comfort zone because of the environment they find themselves in. Some can fall into the trap of thinking they've made it as a Liverpool player because they are training here at Melwood every day. It's up to us to remind them that they are only Liverpool reserve players and until they've made that move from our dressing room to the big dressing room it'll remain that way.

"'Come in and do your best every day', this is what we constantly drum into them. There are millions of people all around the world who'd love to be in their shoes and that should be all the motivation they need to make the most of this unique opportunity they have."

39

Jamie Carragher – Profile

Jamie Carragher is hoping to end years of frustration and hurt by finally helping Liverpool make a sustained challenge for the Barclays Premier League title.

The Reds stalwart, who made his debut for the club back in 1997, feels Liverpool have often flattered to deceive when it comes to making a serious push for title number 19 and is hoping that the 2008-09 season will prove to be different.

"People always talk about us pushing for the league, but to be honest it isn't very often that we've even challenged," he said.

"If we were challenging with 10 or 15 games to go then who knows?

"But just a challenge this season would be nice, to still be in the hunt.

"I think it's only happened once since I've been in the team, when I played a few games under Roy Evans.

"We probably should have won the league but let it slip towards the end.

"But since then we've never even challenged so that's something we're all looking for.

"I'd take a title medal over anything else at the moment because that would make my full set, but I just want to be competitive in the league.

"The aim at the start of every season is to be competitive and to win the title. That's what we have to look at this year."

In recent seasons the Reds could well have gone much closer to ending the long wait for the title had they picked up more points against the other members of the so-called 'big four.'

It is an argument Carra is happy to acknowledge but not one he necessarily agrees with.

"They're big games, but it's not just about beating Manchester United or the other so-called big teams. I don't go along with that," he added.

"Manchester United lost twice to Manchester City which no-one expected so who knows?"

With Daniel Agger now fit-again and Martin Skrtel and Sami Hyypia both vying for a centre back position, Carragher accepts he will face a fight for his place in the starting XI. But he insists it is a challenge he is more than ready for.

Jamie Carragher.............

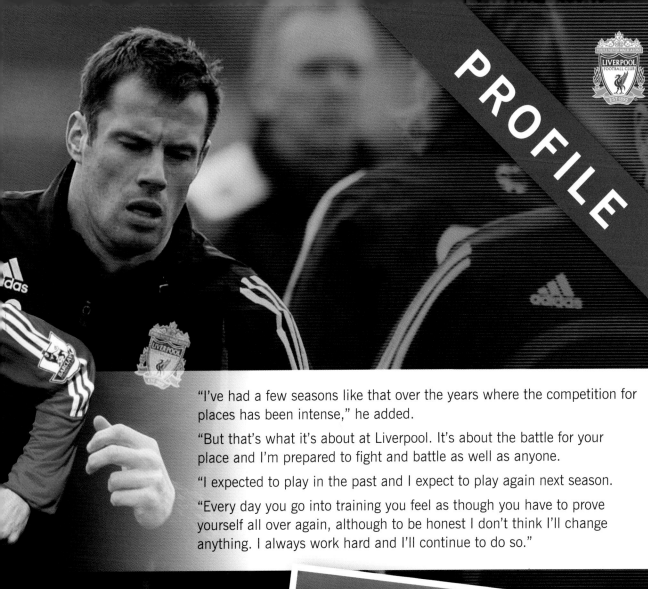

"I've had a few seasons like that over the years where the competition for places has been intense," he added.

"But that's what it's about at Liverpool. It's about the battle for your place and I'm prepared to fight and battle as well as anyone.

"I expected to play in the past and I expect to play again next season.

"Every day you go into training you feel as though you have to prove yourself all over again, although to be honest I don't think I'll change anything. I always work hard and I'll continue to do so."

Jamie Carragher Facts

Date of birth:
28 January 1978

Place of birth:
Bootle, England

Height:
5 ft 10 in (1.78 m)

Playing position:
Centre Back, Full Back

Playing number:
23

41

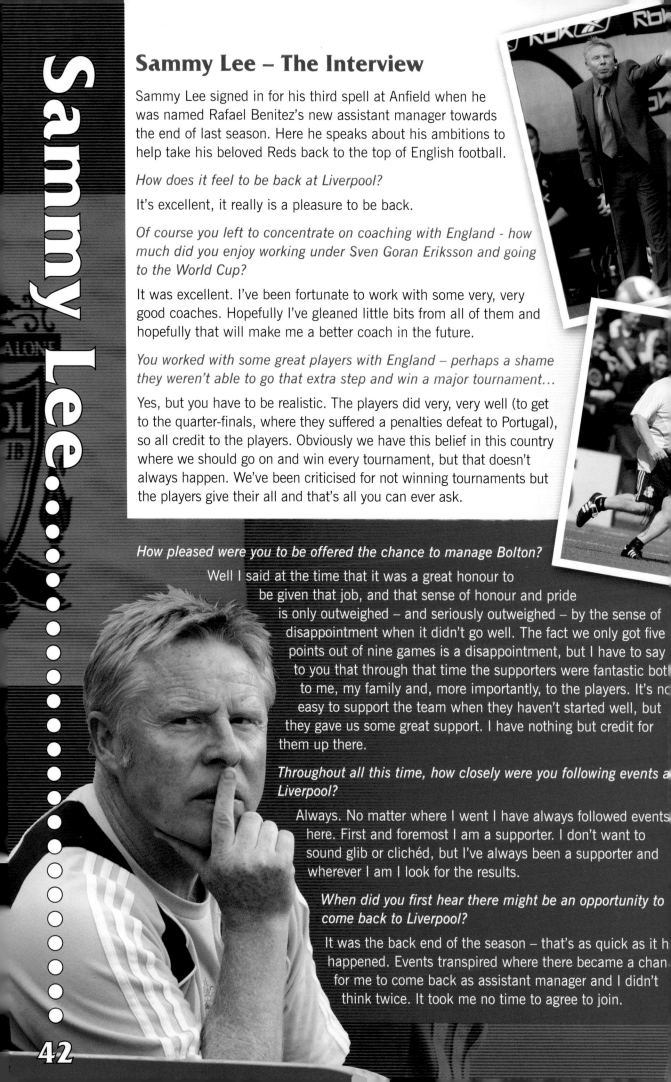

Sammy Lee – The Interview

Sammy Lee signed in for his third spell at Anfield when he was named Rafael Benitez's new assistant manager towards the end of last season. Here he speaks about his ambitions to help take his beloved Reds back to the top of English football.

How does it feel to be back at Liverpool?

It's excellent, it really is a pleasure to be back.

Of course you left to concentrate on coaching with England - how much did you enjoy working under Sven Goran Eriksson and going to the World Cup?

It was excellent. I've been fortunate to work with some very, very good coaches. Hopefully I've gleaned little bits from all of them and hopefully that will make me a better coach in the future.

You worked with some great players with England – perhaps a shame they weren't able to go that extra step and win a major tournament...

Yes, but you have to be realistic. The players did very, very well (to get to the quarter-finals, where they suffered a penalties defeat to Portugal), so all credit to the players. Obviously we have this belief in this country where we should go on and win every tournament, but that doesn't always happen. We've been criticised for not winning tournaments but the players give their all and that's all you can ever ask.

How pleased were you to be offered the chance to manage Bolton?

Well I said at the time that it was a great honour to be given that job, and that sense of honour and pride is only outweighed – and seriously outweighed – by the sense of disappointment when it didn't go well. The fact we only got five points out of nine games is a disappointment, but I have to say to you that through that time the supporters were fantastic both to me, my family and, more importantly, to the players. It's not easy to support the team when they haven't started well, but they gave us some great support. I have nothing but credit for them up there.

Throughout all this time, how closely were you following events at Liverpool?

Always. No matter where I went I have always followed events here. First and foremost I am a supporter. I don't want to sound glib or clichéd, but I've always been a supporter and wherever I am I look for the results.

When did you first hear there might be an opportunity to come back to Liverpool?

It was the back end of the season – that's as quick as it h[as] happened. Events transpired where there became a chan[ce] for me to come back as assistant manager and I didn't think twice. It took me no time to agree to join.

Sammy Lee

Did you just get a phone call from Rafa?

Well believe it or not I'd been here on a study visit. I'd wanted to do one at Liverpool and Rafa told me I could come at the back end of the season. So, by coincidence, I was here for three days last week studying the methods – then the position came up.

You've worked with England and been a Premier League manager since you were last at Liverpool – as well as the study visits. Has all this made you a better coach?

I would hope so. I mention study visits – I did them while I was at the FA as well because I wanted to keep my hand in and broaden my knowledge base. It's important to evolve as a coach. Hopefully all the good experiences and the bad, both as an assistant and a manager, will stand me in good stead for the future.

A lot of fans have said it's great to have a Scouse heart to the coaching staff - you've always had a great rapport with the fans here, haven't you?

Well, I hope so. Basically that's all I am – a Liverpool supporter. You have a certain empathy with them because you eat, drink and sleep Liverpool Football Club. That's what supporters do and that never changes. Hopefully I have empathy with them.

You've worked under Graeme Souness, Roy Evans and Gerard Houllier. The man in charge now is Rafa Benitez. How much are you looking forward to working with Rafa?

Very much. Everyone can see that he's taken this club great strides forward. I am really looking forward to it. You can see his vision from the people he's got here and the people he is trying to bring here. I've been very impressed with him.

Are we far away from being where we want to be once again in the Premier League, in your view?

People may say differently, but I don't think so. It's fine lines in certain games, little things here and there. We aren't far away.

That would be the ultimate for Sammy Lee, wouldn't it? Winning the league…

That's what everyone wants, everyone at this football club, not just Sammy Lee. Everyone who supports this club knows exactly what we want and that's what we're aiming for. We don't aim for anything less than the top spot. We haven't had it for a while, granted, but to aim for anything less would be doing this club a disservice. I can say to you that everyone here has been and is looking forward to getting that number one spot.

After a sensational debut season at Anfield, during which he netted 33 goals, fans on the club's official website were tasked with voting for the best of the bunch from Fernando Torres. With so many to choose from it was always going to be a tough decision - but here are the results:

10: Tottenham v Liverpool May 11 2008

It was a fitting way to end an incredible campaign as Torres signed off with what had become a trademark goal on the final day of the season.

With one drop of the shoulder and a well slotted shot into the far corner, the Reds' marksman had not only secured the points at White Hart Lane but also written himself into the history books by becoming the most prolific foreign goalscorer in a debut season in the Premier League.

9: Derby County v Liverpool December 26 2007

Although most of his goals had come in front of his beloved Anfield crowd, Torres had a habit of saving his very best strikes for games on the road.

His goal at relegation threatened Derby County was a majestic individual strike as he first of all nutmegged a defender before cutting inside onto his left foot and unleashing an unstoppable drive into the far corner of the net.

8: Liverpool v Everton March 30 2008

Selected for its importance rather than its eye-catching quality, this was another example of a big game player delivering the goods when it mattered the most. With fourth place in the league at stake and Everton breathing down Liverpool's necks in the race for the final Champions League qualification place, Torres latched onto a loose ball inside the area before firing low and true into the Kop goal.

7: Liverpool v Middlesbrough February 23 2008

In a surprisingly thrilling contest, Liverpool got the better of their North East opponents thanks to a brace of goals from Torres. In a repeat of his strike earlier in the campaign at the Riverside Stadium, it was a stunning strike from the Spaniard which saw the Reds edge ahead in the game as he collected the ball outside the area and took one step forward before crashing a ferocious shot inside the right hand post of Mark Schwarzer's net.

6: Middlesbrough v Liverpool January 12 2008

His second goal away from Anfield and another to cherish from Liverpool's number nine.
With time running out and Liverpool trailing undeservedly in the game, Torres decided to take matters into his own hands and succeeded in sending the travelling fans wild with delight with a brilliant long range shot which gave the 'keeper no chance as it sailed past him into the roof of the net.

5: Liverpool v Newcastle March 8 2008

Where Pele once failed, Fernando Torres has now succeeded. A goal of quite outstanding brilliance to finish off a glorious move which had the home fans purring with delight.
Once Steven Gerrard had fired the ball into Torres' path, the Spanish star brilliantly dummied the Newcastle goalkeeper out of position with a feint to shoot, but after letting the ball roll past his foot he then had the simple task of guiding his shot into the gaping goal. Brilliant.

4: Inter Milan v Liverpool March 11 2008

And just three days after his strike which sunk the Geordies, Torres set about securing Liverpool a place in the quarter-finals of the Champions League with another wonderful goal to send Inter Milan out of the competition. Needing only a draw to progress at the San Siro, Torres went one better and won the game for the Reds with a fantastic low shot on the turn from outside the area after controlling the ball instantly on his chest.

3: Liverpool v Arsenal April 8 2008

And another Champions League goal on an Anfield night to remember as Torres gave Liverpool a 2-1 lead in a rollercoaster clash on Merseyside. Collecting the ball just inside the area, he brilliantly escaped the shackles of Philip Senderos before driving a rising shot high into the roof of the Kop net. It was another masterful finish from the Reds' main man.

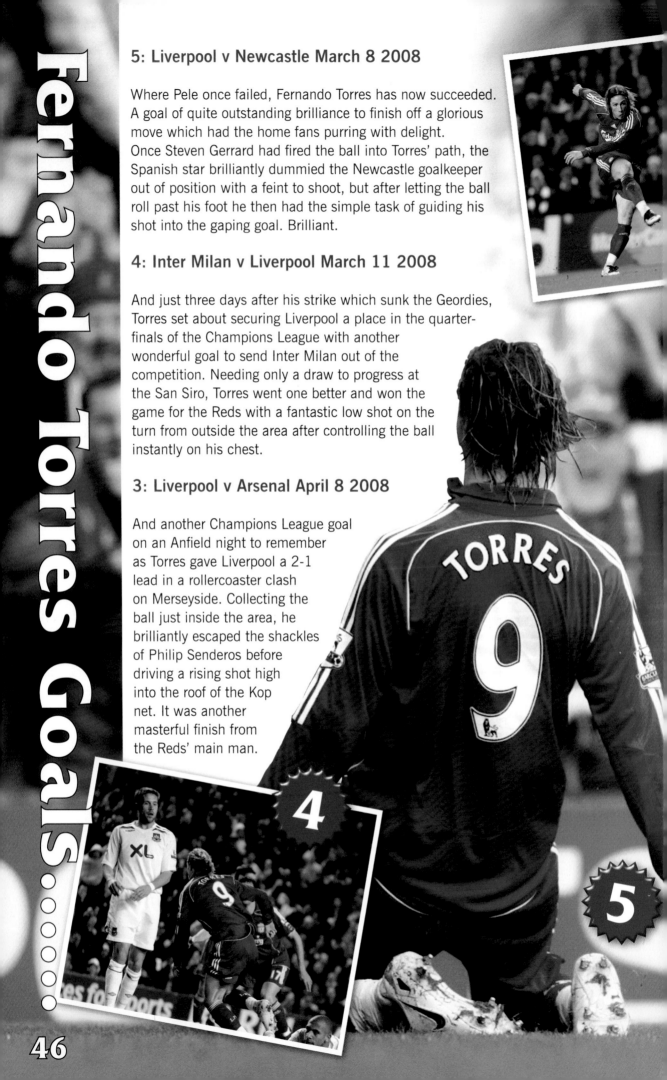

2: Liverpool v Chelsea August 19 2007

What a start to his Anfield career as Torres got off the mark in his first game on his new pitch with a goal of sublime quality. There appeared little danger as he entered the area with Tal Ben Haim for company, but after superbly dragging the ball past his opponent he then calmly stroked the ball past Petr Cech and turned away triumphantly after watching it nestle in the far corner of the goal.

1: Marseille v Liverpool December 11 2007

The runaway winner of Torres' personal goal of the season was scored on an incredible night in the south of France as Liverpool kept their European dreams alive with an emphatic victory over Marseille. The Reds were already ahead on the night but still needed the cushion of a second goal - and it was provided magnificently as Torres dribbled his way past a succession of defenders before finishing in style. A worthy winner to any goal of the season competition!

Javier Mascherano – Profile

Javier Mascherano is determined to use the disappointment felt at Liverpool's failure to capture silverware last season as a positive motivation for the coming campaign.

The Reds saw their Champions League dreams ended by Chelsea last year while in the Premier League a title challenge was never forthcoming - but those setbacks haven't dampened the Argentinean's view of the quality at Anfield.

And he insists it's just a matter of time before Rafael Benitez's vision for his side to be on top of the pile in this country will be realised.

"We are a young team and a team that can win titles," he said. "We know what we're capable of and now it's just a matter of proving it on the field.

Javier Mascherano Facts

Date of birth: **8 June 1984**

Place of birth: **San Lorenzo, Argentina**

Height: **5 ft 9 in (1.75 m)**

Playing position: **Defensive midfielder**

Playing number: **20**

"I think we have shown that on our day we can beat anybody, it's just unfortunate that at times we have dropped silly points or given away silly goals which have ultimately cost us.

"Next season will be very, very different. Next season teams will have to believe in our challenge.

"We have the supporters of a champion team, we have a team of potential champions and who all believe in the same things.

"How can we not achieve our dreams when that is true? We will be back in August more hungry for silverware than ever."

He may be small in stature, but the fact he has been nicknamed 'The Monster' by legendary midfield man Diego Maradona tells you everything you need to know about Mascherano's combative qualities.

"I meet supporters and they tell me this. It makes me happy because it tells me I made the right decision coming to England and coming to Liverpool," he said.

"It shows I am doing the things I need to and doing them right. I am not as tall as Steven (Gerrard) or even as tall as any of the players that I play against. So I need to be brave and prove for every minute of every game that I have a big heart.

"I would say that in my position, because of my size, I have to try twice as hard as the opposition players I am playing against.

"I am the smallest player in the Liverpool team. I am maybe one of the smallest central midfielders in the country and people will, I am sure, look at me before we play them and think that they will be able to dominate me physically.

"I think that in the course of my time at Liverpool I have proved that they can't. I won't let them."

And having turned an initial loan spell into a permanent deal, Mascherano is thrilled to be able to call himself a full time Liverpool player.

"It is a matter of great pride for me to represent the famous name of Liverpool.

"I want to play my part in making this club even more successful. I want to ensure this is the last season without a trophy for a long time."

He added: "I am not finished as a player and I look at the other players in this team and I try to learn things from them.

"But I have definitely had a more consistent season this year than I had in the six months after I first arrived.

"All the time I try to improve, to get better, and like I said already I have learned some things this season."

Philipp Degen – a few words...

How does it feel to be an LFC player?

I feel very good. It's a great club with great fans and I am happy to be here. I know the club has a strong tradition and a rich history. I hope to play a big role in the future.

How much are you looking forward to the challenge of playing in England?

Well, you probably know that I played in Germany with Borussia Dortmund - that was a strong league too. But now I'm looking forward to the challenge of England and the Premier League, which is probably the strongest league in the world right now.

You've been to Anfield before, haven't you?

I have been to Anfield before, with Basel; although I did not play on that occasion. But it was a great experience and to see the fans singing the famous song 'You'll Never Walk Alone' was something special.

What are your main attributes as a player?

I am a pacey player who likes to get forward. I have a good attacking mentality and like to get up and down the flank. I also have good technique.

How important was Rafa in you joining the club?

He was very important. He is the manager here and one of the finest coaches in the world. He has a fantastic record with both LFC and Valencia. I'm looking forward to working with him.

You will face stiff competition from Steve Finnan and Alvaro Arbeloa in the right-back berth...

Yes, I know. They are very good players and it will be difficult but I am ready for the challenge and look forward to breaking into the first team soon.

Can we challenge for the league?

I am sure we can challenge. We have a very strong team with the likes of Steven Gerrard and Fernando Torres. But there are some strong opponents in Man Utd and Chelsea, so we will have to be very consistent. It's a long season and anything can happen but we will go into the first game of the campaign hoping to push them all the way.

Finally, a message for the fans?

I will do all I can for the side and for the fans. I want the club to succeed and I will always do my best to ensure Liverpool are winning matches.

5 facts on our new boy:

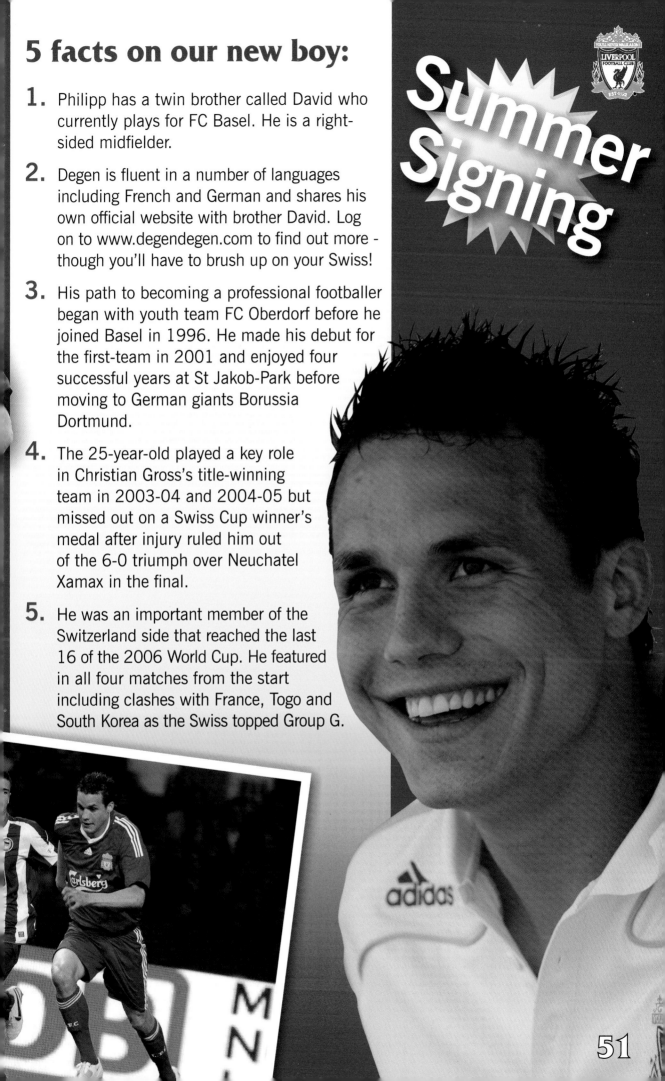

1. Philipp has a twin brother called David who currently plays for FC Basel. He is a right-sided midfielder.

2. Degen is fluent in a number of languages including French and German and shares his own official website with brother David. Log on to www.degendegen.com to find out more - though you'll have to brush up on your Swiss!

3. His path to becoming a professional footballer began with youth team FC Oberdorf before he joined Basel in 1996. He made his debut for the first-team in 2001 and enjoyed four successful years at St Jakob-Park before moving to German giants Borussia Dortmund.

4. The 25-year-old played a key role in Christian Gross's title-winning team in 2003-04 and 2004-05 but missed out on a Swiss Cup winner's medal after injury ruled him out of the 6-0 triumph over Neuchatel Xamax in the final.

5. He was an important member of the Switzerland side that reached the last 16 of the 2006 World Cup. He featured in all four matches from the start including clashes with France, Togo and South Korea as the Swiss topped Group G.

Summer Signing

Andrea Dossena – a few words...

New signing Andrea Dossena claims Liverpool have bought an Italian defender with an English heart.

The 27-year-old left-back hopes a combination of determination and quality on the ball will make his transition from Serie A to the Premier League an easy one.

He admits training at Melwood is faster than what he is used to but insists his 'half-English, half Italian' style will see him through.

"Even from training I realise English football is different," he said.

"It's all about possession and the ball seems to move quicker. There is also a great determination among the players in training, but these are all qualities that are characteristic of me too. In this way, I feel half English, half Italian."

Dossena is seen as a direct replacement for the outgoing John Arne Riise, who travelled in the opposite direction after signing for Roma.

Rafa Benitez has already revealed how both the left-back and fellow new boy Philipp Degen are ready to go straight into the first team – words that are music to the ears of a man desperate to pull on a red jersey for the first time.

"It is an honour to be wearing such a prestigious shirt." said Dossena. "It was great for me that Liverpool were so determined to have me in their squad. It is a very important shirt to wear and I will do my best. I have a great will to work hard and succeed and achieve great results.

"Of course I'll feel very strong emotions when I wear the shirt at Anfield for the first time but after the first few seconds these will be replaced by a focus on what I am doing.

"There are so many great players here and I hope to be playing beside them as soon as possible.

"I believe I will bring determination as my main strength. I have a will to succeed and achieve results. These are also characteristics I have seen in Liverpool as a team."

His new boss is one of very few Italian speakers at the club, but the defender claims his broken English is getting him by with the likes of Jamie Carragher.

"I have been able to talk to my team-mates but of course I have had to talk a little slower and maybe they have too, so they understand me better," he said.

"I have been very impressed with the facilities and also with the very good atmosphere in the dressing room.

"The talks I have had with Benitez have mostly been about tactics. He has explained that he wants a four-man defence but that the most important thing is that the balance on the pitch is never broken. There must be balance between the left and right-backs."

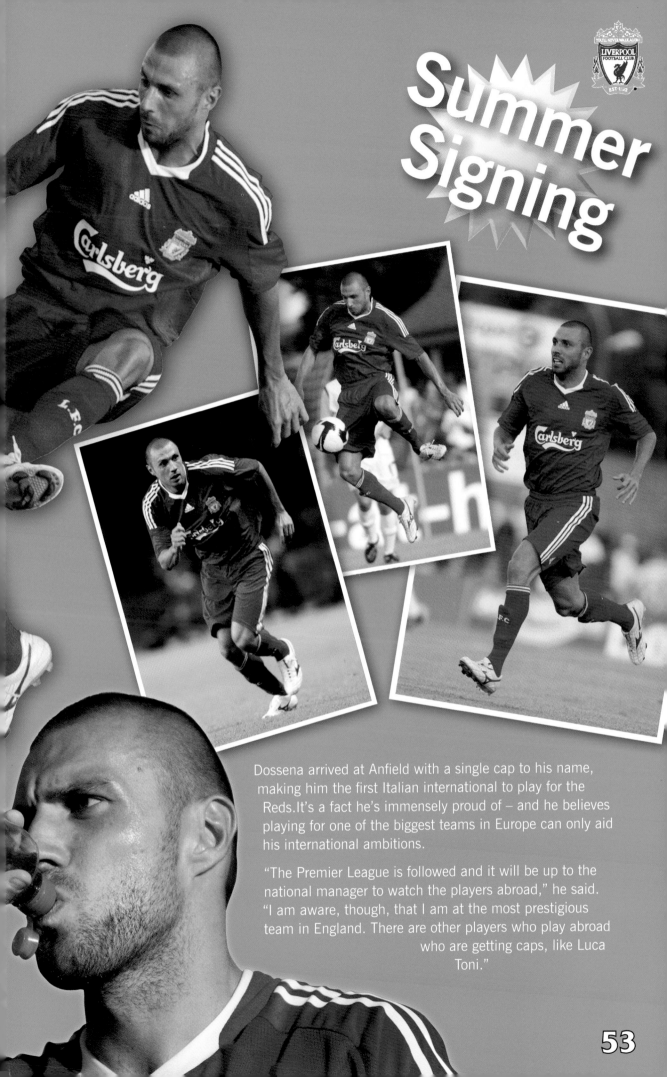

Summer Signing

Dossena arrived at Anfield with a single cap to his name, making him the first Italian international to play for the Reds. It's a fact he's immensely proud of – and he believes playing for one of the biggest teams in Europe can only aid his international ambitions.

"The Premier League is followed and it will be up to the national manager to watch the players abroad," he said. "I am aware, though, that I am at the most prestigious team in England. There are other players who play abroad who are getting caps, like Luca Toni."

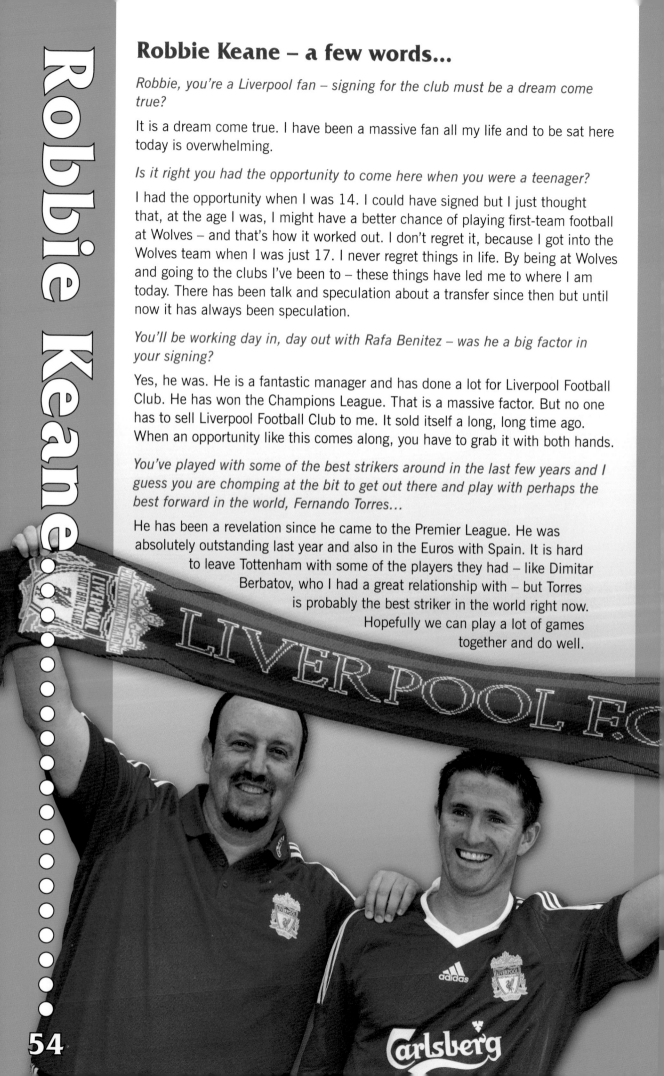

Robbie Keane – a few words...

Robbie, you're a Liverpool fan – signing for the club must be a dream come true?

It is a dream come true. I have been a massive fan all my life and to be sat here today is overwhelming.

Is it right you had the opportunity to come here when you were a teenager?

I had the opportunity when I was 14. I could have signed but I just thought that, at the age I was, I might have a better chance of playing first-team football at Wolves – and that's how it worked out. I don't regret it, because I got into the Wolves team when I was just 17. I never regret things in life. By being at Wolves and going to the clubs I've been to – these things have led me to where I am today. There has been talk and speculation about a transfer since then but until now it has always been speculation.

You'll be working day in, day out with Rafa Benitez – was he a big factor in your signing?

Yes, he was. He is a fantastic manager and has done a lot for Liverpool Football Club. He has won the Champions League. That is a massive factor. But no one has to sell Liverpool Football Club to me. It sold itself a long, long time ago. When an opportunity like this comes along, you have to grab it with both hands.

You've played with some of the best strikers around in the last few years and I guess you are chomping at the bit to get out there and play with perhaps the best forward in the world, Fernando Torres...

He has been a revelation since he came to the Premier League. He was absolutely outstanding last year and also in the Euros with Spain. It is hard to leave Tottenham with some of the players they had – like Dimitar Berbatov, who I had a great relationship with – but Torres is probably the best striker in the world right now. Hopefully we can play a lot of games together and do well.

Do you see yourself as a second striker, someone who can play a bit deeper behind, say, Torres, or as a striker in your own right?

I see myself as a second striker. I can play off the shoulder, link things up and play in the hole. You are always judged on scoring goals as a striker and I have always scored a lot of goals. Hopefully I can continue that here at Liverpool.

Was the lure of the Champions League a big factor?

I have only played in Champions League qualifiers before but, you know, it's the whole package. I have always wanted to come here but, yes, the Champions League and being able to win things is a major factor.

At 28, would you say you are in your prime?

Yes, I think so. The last four years have been great for me and I believe I am at my peak. I am at a good age and if I didn't come to Liverpool now, maybe the opportunity wouldn't come again. It has worked out perfectly for me and, hopefully, for Liverpool Football Club as well.

You are famous for your cartwheel celebration – might we see that at Anfield any time soon?

I will probably bring it out once for the Liverpool fans as I've done it down the years, but after that it will probably go back in the box.

And this must be a nice way to end a brilliant summer for you, what with you getting married as well?

Yes, it's been a fantastic year for me all in all, with Tottenham doing well and winning the League Cup, then getting married and now coming to the club I love. I will never, ever forget this year.

Summer Signing

Pepe Reina – The Interview

After collecting the Barclays Premier League's Golden Glove award for most clean sheets in a season for the third year running, we spoke to Pepe Reina about the latest addition to his trophy collection...

These are coming around regularly now, Pepe...

Yes, well the team has been defending so good for three years. It's not about me. It's about the team working together, the work rate of all of us. I have said it many, many times and I will say it again – these awards are for the team, it's just that I get to keep it at home.

You're modest but you must be very proud, because goalkeepers don't always get the recognition they deserve, do they?

Sometimes we don't, but as a goalkeeper you know and have to accept that you are recognised more for your mistakes than your saves. For us it's normal, so it is nice to take these kind of trophies home and look at them from the sofa.

Yes, where do you put them all – are you running out of space?

I don't know. They will go with the other two so I can show friends when they come round.

Being Liverpool goalkeeper is often about keeping your concentration because you may only have one or two saves to make. Do you prefer it like this or would you like the chance to show off a bit more?

No, I like it how it is. The fewer saves the better because it means the team is winning and giving our rivals fewer chances to score. At a big club this is how it is. There are two or three saves to make and that's your responsibility.
I like this responsibility.

We'd ask Stevie or Fernando their favourite goal last season – how about you, which of your 18 clean sheets has meant the most?

It's difficult. Any clean sheet is important. If you were to ask me about saves I would say the one I made against Bolton. That was good and important because the score was 0-0 or 1-0.

We've also seen a few assists from you this year, most memorably against Fulham at home. Talk us through that...

It was a clearance to be honest! But no, it was a long kick which Fernando got and he finished it for himself. I was very pleased because it was a goal but it was more about Fernando than my pass.

Rafa Benitez's view on the Reds' undisputed number one:

"Pepe is a 'keeper in a top side, so he has less to do. If he played for a lesser team he would be fantastic because he'd be involved all the time. He is a very good goalkeeper.

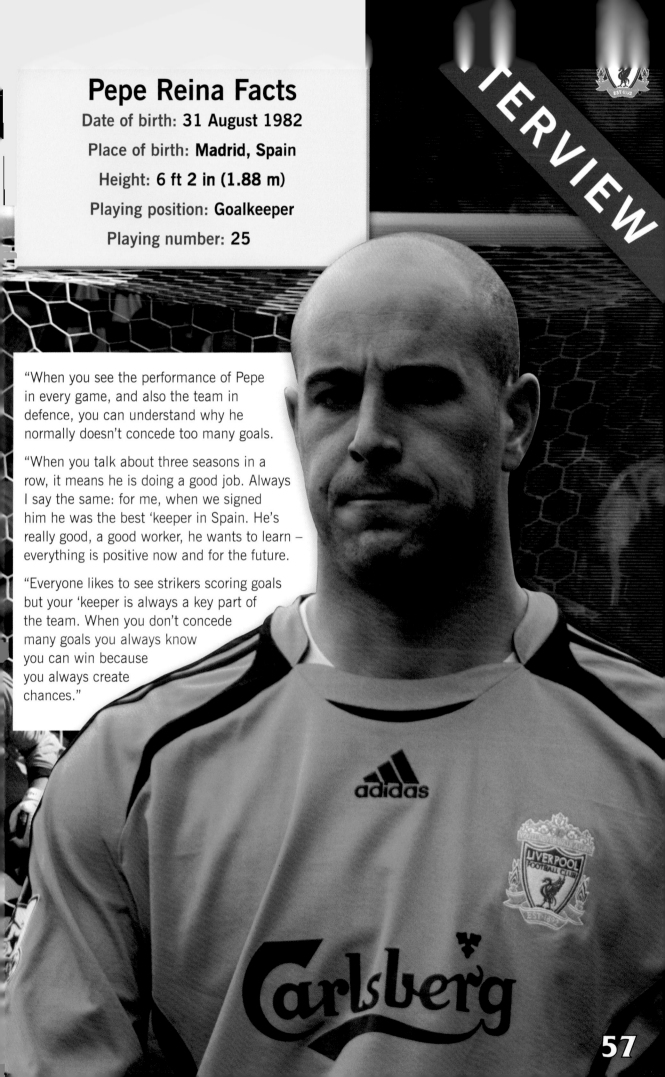

Pepe Reina Facts

Date of birth: **31 August 1982**

Place of birth: **Madrid, Spain**

Height: **6 ft 2 in (1.88 m)**

Playing position: **Goalkeeper**

Playing number: **25**

"When you see the performance of Pepe in every game, and also the team in defence, you can understand why he normally doesn't concede too many goals.

"When you talk about three seasons in a row, it means he is doing a good job. Always I say the same: for me, when we signed him he was the best 'keeper in Spain. He's really good, a good worker, he wants to learn – everything is positive now and for the future.

"Everyone likes to see strikers scoring goals but your 'keeper is always a key part of the team. When you don't concede many goals you always know you can win because you always create chances."

Dirk Kuyt – The Interview

Dirk Kuyt is relishing the challenge of continuing to establish himself as Liverpool's wide man for the big occasion.

Despite having arrived at Anfield as a free scoring, out and out goalscorer - and despite an impressive goals return during his early months at Anfield - the Dutch international has since made a name for himself on the right side of the Reds' midfield where he has been able to combine his relentless workrate with a happy knack of arriving at the right time in the area to poach vital goals.

Some strikers may complain about their unhappiness at being switched from their so-called favourite position - but Kuyt admits he's just thrilled to have such an important role to play in Liverpool's first team plans.

"I don't really like to be put in any specific bracket, a right midfielder, right winger, striker or second striker," Kuyt said.

"I've probably got a bit of all these positions within my game. I can play as a striker, a second striker or on the right or on the left. Whatever that may be, I just like to do it my own way.

"But playing on the right is not exactly new to me. I've played there for two years in the Dutch national team and also for a year-and-a-half when I started out at Utrecht. I know what to do out there so it's not like I'm just learning the job.

"In this new role I have to work really hard in both attack and defence. Instead of always looking to get on the end of them I'm now always looking to provide crosses for the other strikers.

"There are still chances for me to score but probably not as many as if I was playing in the centre. I'm quite happy with my performances since I've been out there. I've scored a few goals as well as provided assists and so I feel it's going well.

"I always keep an eye on my assists. As I say, they are just as important to me and I've had quite a few so far. I've probably got about five or six assists since I've been out on the right, which isn't a bad tally.

"No matter where I play, I like to work really hard for the team with the same main target of helping us win as many games as possible. That is what it is all about.

"I was happy to be the top scorer in Holland and to be named Player of the Season there but I would hand all of these personal awards back to win the league or one of the cups here with Liverpool.

"It's a team sport and you win things together. That's what I like about football."

And Kuyt is especially keen to help the Reds land more glory to help pay back boss Rafa Benitez who stuck

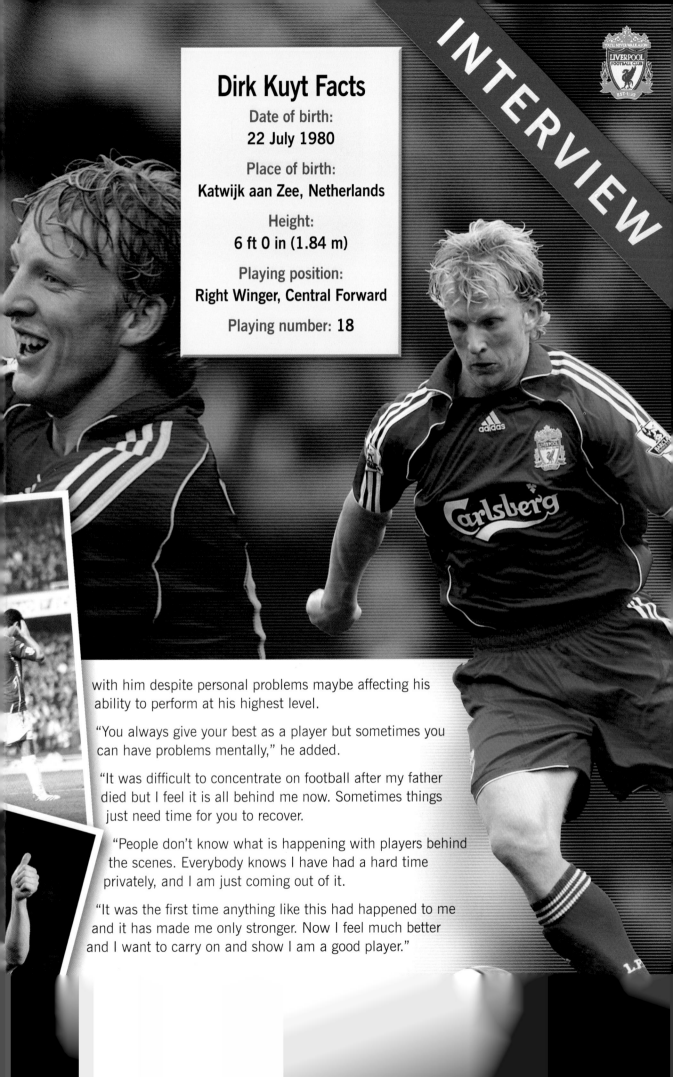

Dirk Kuyt Facts

Date of birth:
22 July 1980

Place of birth:
Katwijk aan Zee, Netherlands

Height:
6 ft 0 in (1.84 m)

Playing position:
Right Winger, Central Forward

Playing number: **18**

with him despite personal problems maybe affecting his ability to perform at his highest level.

"You always give your best as a player but sometimes you can have problems mentally," he added.

"It was difficult to concentrate on football after my father died but I feel it is all behind me now. Sometimes things just need time for you to recover.

"People don't know what is happening with players behind the scenes. Everybody knows I have had a hard time privately, and I am just coming out of it.

"It was the first time anything like this had happened to me and it has made me only stronger. Now I feel much better and I want to carry on and show I am a good player."

Answers for quiz on pages 30-31. Check you answers to see how well you did. Did you get them all right?

Q 01. From which club did Liverpool sign Fernando Torres?
A. Atletico Madrid

Q 02. Against which side did Ryan Babel score his first Liverpool goal?
A. Derby County

Q 03. Who returned to the coaching staff at the end of last season as assistant manager?
A. Sammy Lee

Q 04. And who did he replace in that role?
A. Pako Ayestaran

Q 05. How many goals did Steven Gerrard score last season?
A. 21

Q 06. Against which side did Fernando Torres score his first hat-trick for the Reds?
A. Reading

Q 07. What number does Daniel Agger wear at Anfield?
A. 5

Q 08. What nationality is Lucas Leiva?
A. Brazilian

Q 09. How many games did Liverpool lose in the Premier League last season?
A. 4

Q 10. Who scored an own goal in the Champions League semi-final first leg clash at Anfield
A. John Arne Riise

Q 11. What was the overall aggregate score in the tie after the second leg?
A. 3-4

Q 12. Who wears the number 20 shirt at the club?
A. Javier Mascherano

Q 13. And which country does this player come from?
A. Argentina

Q 14. Which side knocked us out of the FA Cup last season?
A. Barnsley

Q 15. Who scored for Liverpool in that game?
A. Dirk Kuyt

Q 16. How many players did we have representing us in the Spanish squad at Euro 2008?
A. Four. Alvaro Arbeloa, Xabi Alonso, Pepe Reina and Fernando Torres

Q 17. Who is the manager of the Liverpool reserve side?
A. Gary Ablett

Q 18. Where did Liverpool's reserves play their home games last season?
A. Warrington Wolves

Q 19. What is Liverpool's training ground called?
A. Melwood

Q 20. How many goals did Fernando Torres score in his first season in England?
A. 33

Answers for
Spot the Difference
on page 18.
How well did
you do. Did you
spot all of them?

Solution for
Spot the Ball page 19.
Did you find it?